THE FAMILY LAW GUIDE TO APPELLATE PRACTICE

MATTHEW P. BARACH

ABA
SECTION OF FAMILY LAW

Cover design by Kelly Book/ABA Design.

Printed in the United States of America.

23 22 21 20 19 5 4 3 2 1

Library of Congress Cataloging-in-Publication Notice
Names: Barach, Matthew P., author.
Title: The family law guide to appellate practice / Matthew P. Barach.
Description: Chicago : American Bar Association, 2019.
Identifiers: LCCN 2018050762 (print) | LCCN 2018050860 (ebook) | ISBN 9781641053570 (ebook) | ISBN 9781641053563 (pbk.)
Subjects: LCSH: Domestic relations courts—United States. | Domestic relations—United States. | Appellate procedure—United States.
Classification: LCC KF505.5 (ebook) | LCC KF505.5 .B37 2019 (print) | DDC 346.7301/50269—dc23
LC record available at https://lccn.loc.gov/2018050762

For my father, who shared with me
his great love of books.

Contents

Preface

Family law matters are intimate, personal, and touch upon people's most private treasurers. This perspective directly affects all aspects of domestic relations, including appellate practice. As a result, family law appeals provide certain dilemmas not existing in other areas of the practice of law.

If this book has an underlying purpose—besides serving as a practical guide for a novice to appeal a family court decision—then it is for you to be both cautious and extraordinarily careful in choosing to appeal a family law case.

You must consider the potential result and costs both on individual lives and on the precedent a matter could set upon future litigants, including your own.

As an old sage once advised, "There is an equal chance of creating bad law as good law when you appeal."

Do not jump in.

But rather wade in and determine whether the choice to appeal is both proper and wise. The context matters. You are dealing with people's most intimate concerns, emotions, minds, and hearts. Take good care of them. Try always to inflict no harm upon them.

Words are powerful. Use them carefully and with due caution.

Words move mountains, alter lives, and change ordinary people into heroes. A well-crafted story is impactful long after it has been read. A powerful argument may change a mind and make a difference in the world. Your ability to persuade a judge or a panel of jurists will live long after you.

I hope you use these words in the pages ahead wisely. I hope you are impactful, make a difference, and are always extraordinary in your representation of all of your clients.

Matthew P. Barach, Esq.

A Note About Sources

I relied on a number of major and minor sources in creating this book for the family law appellate advocate. The major sources include Appellate Practice in Federal and State Courts, the ABA Section of Family Law, *Family Advocate*, Spring 2014 Vol. 36, No. 4, which was devoted to appeals for family law attorneys; *Making Your Case: The Art of Persuading Judges* by the late justice Antonin Scalia and his writing partner Bryan A. Garner; and *A Practical Guide to Appellate Advocacy* by Mary Beth Beazley. The chapter devoted to the reply brief was adopted from a terrific article on reply briefs from the American Bar Association litigation section by Damon Thayer.

These fine writings are liberally utilized and adapted into a family law attorney's perspective for a better understanding of the material. I am indebted to all of the authors of these excellent works for making my job easier and am grateful these works came before my own so I was able to rely upon them in this creation.

Minor sources include *The Little Book on Oral Argument* by Alan L. Dworsky, *Appellate Practice Manual* by Priscilla Anne Schwab, and *Trying Divorce Cases in Massachusetts* by my colleague Donald Tye. The latter was particularly helpful, as it contains a very good exploration of post-trial motions, which can be adapted to any jurisdiction. I relied on a number of other law journal articles, numerous state and federal statutes, and state guides to appellate practice.

I fully credit the authors of all these materials for assisting me in the creation of what comes next and thank them all for their valuable contribution.

Introduction

There are many terrific books and sources on how to appeal both criminal and civil matters. Strangely, books dedicated to the art and/or science of appellate practice for the *family law advocate only* do not exist. If this book were a legal issue, it would be one of first impression. It is designed to fill the void in family law materials.

As you are aware, family law raises unique concerns and issues differing from other areas of law practice. This guide assists you on the "nuts and bolts" of handling a family law appeal.

The pages ahead are specifically crafted as a "how to note" to the family law attorney, or a pro se litigant, who receives an adverse decision and wants to appeal the matter but requires some proper guidance.

The early chapters focus on the crucial decision to appeal and factors involved, including ethical considerations. We then examine the effective use of post-trial remedies, such as utilizing stays of judgments pending appeals, and creating, protecting, and reviewing the record of the trial court.

The middle chapters explore understanding appellate standards of review, appealing interlocutory issues, drafting and filing the notice of appeal and assembly of the record, learning the importance of the Record Appendix, preparing to write a brief, using authorities, drafting techniques and considerations, formatting a brief correctly, and using style effectively.

We then move to writing a persuasive brief, including the perspective of an appellant versus an appellee, and we look at the reply brief. We then begin our exploration of oral argument.

The last chapters focus on the expectations and importance of an oral argument. We cover preparing, presenting, and handling panel questions of the various types of jurists and end with the aftermath of an appellate decision.

Materials are adapted from civil law appellate practice books, guides, articles on various aspects of the appellate process, and federal and state statutes concerning appellate rules and procedures.

I liberally adapt source material specifically for the family law attorney and provide numerous examples when appropriate to emphasize issues on appeal in domestic relations. There are from the trenches a number of helpful practice pointers along the way. The first rule is:

PRACTICE POINTER

You must know your local rules of appellate practice in your jurisdiction.

There is no substitute for understanding your own local rules. Use this guide to enable your application of those rules in your own jurisdiction. I strongly encourage you to read local briefs and watch family law appellate oral arguments.

As indicated, there are various considerations in appellate practice in the pages ahead, but I have specifically not provided a full brief, as I leave it to your own creation. However, the tools ahead enable you to file your own strong and hopefully successful brief.

You can certainly read this book cover to cover, but do not feel compelled to do so. Use the chapters on an "as needed basis" for a specific understanding of what you are facing when confronted with a family law appeal.

I hope it is helpful and enables you to produce excellent appellant submissions for your clients and reach greater heights in your own practice of family law.

> *Excellence is never an accident. It is always the result of high intention, sincere effort, and intelligent execution; it represents the wise choice of many alternatives—choice, not chance determines your destiny.*
>
> —Aristotle

> *I know of no higher fortitude than stubbornness in the face of overwhelming odds.*
>
> —Louis Nizer, Esq.

The Decision to Appeal 1

The trial is long over. Months pass and dust begins to collect on your trial binder and exhibit books. Post-trial submissions sit silently in the corner of your office. Suddenly, in the middle of a very busy and long day, a large, ominous manila folder arrives from the trial court: the judgment.

Your heart begins to pound heavily while your muscles start to quiver and shake. You hastily open it. You immediately skip to the conclusion. You read it. You read it again. You put it down. You think, *Is this what we had proposed in our post-trial submissions to the court? This does not seem very familiar.*

You race to the corner of your office to find your post-trial folder, skimming it briefly as your heart pounds. Is this result even close to our proposed judgment? Wait. What the heck? Is this decision from your case? It cannot be.

So you go back again and you read it again. You start at the beginning. You read carefully. You then go back to the judgment itself. You stop. You scan your file and read your post-trial submissions, now comparing them to the actual judgment. You do not like what you see. You reach for a glass of water. You think of the client. Again, you think, *What the heck?* You take a long, deep breath.

This is not what we were seeking at all. This must be an error, a mistake, a bad dream. This is not even close to what we had proposed. My poor client. This is not right. Unfair. Unreasonable. An injustice. I need to do something. I must do something. I must appeal!!

A. WHAT IS AN APPEAL?

First, what *really* is an appeal? The word *appeal* is defined as an "earnest or urgent request."[1] This is an insightful definition for the family law advocate and one to keep in mind as you analyze the decision *to appeal*.

Clients appeal adverse rulings when they are unhappy with the results. They seek justice and to show the world they are in the right and his or her ex-spouse is in the wrong. They are angry with the judge who they believe made the wrong decision. Clients wish to show the judge how "stupid" the decision is in his or her case. But the motivation "to win" or to correct a perceived injustice is not enough to seek an appeal from a reviewing court. There are numerous considerations to review prior to filing an appeal.

From a functional perspective, the appeal is a proceeding to allow a higher court to review a lower court's decision. But appellate courts review only those issues actually presented to the trial court—the record—so long as they are preserved for appellate review.[2] You must specifically identify errors actually decided and committed by the trial court or you lose your appeal. Any issue not brought before the lower court is lost. In addition, statistically very few appeals succeed.

The result of an appeal of a family law decision can vary. You can lose. Worse, you can lose with an award of legal fees to the other party. A very nasty result for your client.

---

1. *Appeal,* World Web Online, http://www.wordwebonline.com (last visited November 1, 2017).

2. Singleton v. Wulff, 428 U.S. 106, 119–21 (1976).

Or, as often happens in family law cases, the matter is remanded for further proceedings to correct the errors found within the trial court's judgment. This can happen, even when an appellate court finds a legal error was made; the court may simply return the case back to the trial court to reconsider its other rulings in light of the appellate court's decision on the meaning of the law as applied to the facts in your case.

There, you end up back to square one. Ugh.

The reality is that an appeal is not an easy process, odds are high against its success, and most lawyers do not handle or even bother to touch appellate work.

There are a number of ethical obligations as the matter turns from judgment to the possibility of an appeal, starting with the duty to explain to your already agitated client the very long odds against the success of an appeal. Never an easy conversation with your client.

Your client needs to understand that an appeal is not a retrial of the facts or issues, but rather an opportunity to raise mistakes of fact or errors of law by the judge to a reviewing court. Another potentially complicated discussion.

Family law presents particular concerns differing from other areas of the law when it comes to the appellate process.

The impact upon the children is also an important consideration.

The fact that the judgment may not be "stayed" during the pendency of the appeal is another.

The point of a divorce is "moving on," and an appeal can further elongate emotions and increase the acrimony rather than deescalate the matter and provide a client closure.

Family law attorneys are faced with a number of practical challenges in choosing whether to file an appeal. An appeal is more complex than showing the judge got it "wrong" in your case.

The decision of whether to appeal or not to appeal involves evaluating complex factors, including alternative remedies, the likelihood of success, the costs involved, and a determination of what "success" or "failure" on appeal actually means for your client.

You need a complete understanding of not only the mechanics and process of an appeal, but also how to evaluate when it is sensible to bring an "urgent plea" forward.

Let's begin there.

B. APPEALS ARE JUST DIFFERENT IN FAMILY LAW

Family law is intimately personal, unique, exceptional, and factually based.[3] The facts are critical in each family law matter. Family law judges are closest to the "action" of the parties. As a result, appellate courts afford broad discretion to the trial judge when reviewing family law judgments.

A careful and thorough examination of the facts is necessary to determine whether to appeal or not to appeal.

Often, there are as many good reasons not to challenge a judgment as reasons to pursue a reversal or remand of a trial judgment. Fortunately, there are a few alternatives to seeking an appeal that in some circumstances can be a better choice.

C. POST-TRIAL MOTIONS BEFORE AN APPEAL

If you are unhappy with a judgment following trial, family courts provide several means for you to take the matter before the trial court again to correct the perceived mistakes rather than appeal. Consider first any post-trial motions prior to the filing of an appeal. These post-trial modifications may include:

- A motion to amend findings of fact.[4]
- A motion to amend conclusions of law.[5]
- A motion for a new trial.[6]
- A motion to amend judgments.[7]
- A motion for relief from judgment and order.[8]
- A motion for reconsideration.[9]
- A motion to modify a judgment based on material changes in the circumstances (if allowed by your jurisdiction).

3. Meredith J. Harbach, *Is the Family a Federal Question*, 66 Wash. & Lee L. Rev. 131, 134 (2009).
4. Generally, Federal Rule of Civil Procedure 52.
5. *Id.*
6. Generally, Federal Rule of Civil Procedure 59.
7. *Id.*
8. Generally, Federal Rule of Civil Procedure Rule 60.
9. If allowed by your local rule.

PRACTICE POINTER

Understand the effect of a post-trial motion on the notice of appeal to preserve your client's appellate rights.

There are highly specific requirements that apply to post-judgment motions, and you need to review your applicable state law post-trial to determine the appropriate steps to file such motions. There may be additional state remedies post-trial available within your local rules. Be familiar with the effect of filing these motions on your client's appellate rights. These motions are further examined in Chapter 6.

D. MODIFICATION

Family law is somewhat unusual, as many "final" orders are subject to modification based on material changes in circumstances. Child support and parenting time orders are two good examples.

Judgments can be "modified" in the future by showing a significant change in circumstance by the same judge who issued the initial order, depending on the local rules of your jurisdiction.

As a result, when your unhappy client is looking at a two- or three-year timeline for an appeal to run through the higher courts, the initial question is whether a post-judgment modification filed during that time frame is a better remedy than an appeal for your client.

For example, a modification rather than an appeal is the correct choice if the real area of dissatisfaction is the claimed unworkability of the orders. A parenting plan that your client is unhappy with is an excellent example.

On the other hand, if the error is an issue of law, the correct remedy is an appeal to a higher court. Higher courts are more interested in issues of law than in factual disputes between parties.

PRACTICE POINTER

If a future modification solves the post-trial problem, it is likely a better avenue than an appeal due to the long odds against a successful appeal.

E. EQUITY ACTIONS

Family law courts are of equitable jurisdiction. These local courts sometimes afford litigants special rules to allow a matter to be brought under principles of equitable fairness—for example, a client who discovers, only after the divorce judgment, his former wife owns a vacation home. States may allow an "equity action" to divide the undisclosed asset. An equity action to divide the undiscovered vacation home is a better option than seeking an appeal in the appellate court.

F. CONSIDERATIONS

Once you determine there is an alternative to an appeal, assess the practical realities of an appeal of your client's case. First, it is a universal rule of appellate practice that the odds of success are never in your client's favor.

In family law cases, the odds of appellate success may be even more stacked against you and your client. Appellate courts simply afford great deference to the trial judge who heard the matter.

G. THE GOAL

Keeping the broad discretion granted trial courts firmly in your mind, pay particular attention to your goal in filing an appeal for your client. The threshold questions are: What does your client hope to accomplish by filing an appeal? Will an appeal make things better or worse for your client? Your client's goal dictates the choice of whether to appeal.

For example, a decision to appeal a minor matter, such as the hours of a child–parent exchange in a child custody judgment, might make a client appear "petty" to the trial judge—the same trial judge who may remember this petty action when the client brings a modification action on a more pressing issue in the future.

It is important to be clear and realistic with your client about the possibilities, the difficulties, the costs, the challenges, and even the statistical chances of achieving an appellate objective. On some occasions, the client may simply need to settle the case.

The next questions to ask: Are your client's goals realistic? Does an appeal stand a chance in the face of the broad discretion granted family court judges? The short answer is many times the goal is likely unachievable.

Practice Pointer

Appeals are more successful when the goals of the client and attorney align.

H. THE COSTS

An important consideration for a client is the costs of an appeal. It is critical to be honest and open with your client regarding the costs and expenses of a possible appeal. It is not enough to simply explore the possible outcomes and challenges of an appeal. It is critical to have a detailed conversation with your client regarding the actual costs an appeal of the matter may entail.

The costs of an appeal include the filing fees, record assembly, trial transcripts, production of the record, and assembly of the brief. These expenses need to be factored in along with the legal costs for you to write research and argue the brief. As a result, the costs of an appeal are both real and substantial and should be weighed with your client against the odds of potential success.

In addition, jurisdictions allow appellate courts to order fees against the party who brought an unsuccessful appeal. An appeal that is in bad faith or meritless may result in not only the sting of losing again, but also the additional pain of paying for the opposing party's costs incurred by the appeal. Ouch.

I. MOOTNESS

Likewise, the challenged judgment remains in place during the pendency of the action. For example, a child's parenting plan remains the same during the appeal.

As children grow and develop during the pendency of a matter, these changes can have a substantial impact on what transpires over and above the appeal. For example, an older child may reach an age where her voice may be heard in a new action. Also, a child could reach the age of emancipation and an appeal may become moot.

Interestingly, the U.S. Supreme Court in *Chafin v. Chafin*[10] addressed the issue of "mootness" in the context of a child custody matter presented under the Hague Convention.

The father, a member of the U.S. military, married the mother, who was from Germany, where she gave birth to the parties' daughter. While the father was later deployed, the mother took their daughter to Scotland, but later re-joined him in Alabama.

Thereafter, the father filed for divorce in an Alabama court, after the mother was deported. She subsequently filed a petition under the Hague Convention, to return her daughter to Scotland.

The district court granted the Mother's petition. The Eleventh Circuit dismissed the father's appeal as moot because the mother had already moved her daughter to Scotland. The Supreme Court reversed the decision.

The Court held a case becomes moot only when it is impossible for a court to grant any effectual relief whatever to the prevailing party. As a result, so long as parties have *some concrete interest in the matter, however minute,* the case is not considered moot. Thus, in the context of a child custody dispute, where a parent has a legal right or interest involving a child, a case may never be considered moot.

J. TIMING

Although a case may not technically become "moot," timing is an important consideration. Sometimes, particularly where the facts are not sympathetic to your client, the emotional toll requires an end to litigation. A "cooling off" period is effective for parties in family law.

An appeal to family law courts may take at least a year and often longer, depending upon the docket of your local jurisdiction.

---

10. Chafin v. Chafin, 568 U.S. 165 (2013).

You and your client must perform a diligent, careful cost-benefit analysis, factoring in the time necessary for an appeal prior to pressing forward.

K. THE REALISTIC CHANCE OF SUCCESS

An obvious consideration is to have an initial candid assessment of the likelihood of an appeal's success. Consider what success or failure may mean to your client after the appeal and what might happen on disputed matters while the appeal is under way.

Ask the following:

Is this a case that *should* be won on appeal?
Do the facts of your case reflect an injustice in the outcome?
Does the result require a remand or even a reversal?
Has the trial judge made a critical mistake in her application of the law to the facts?
Does your gut instinct tell you something is wrong?

Both the facts and the equities need to exhibit that something went very wrong in the trial court. Ideally, by the time an appellate judge reads your statement of facts, even giving the appellee any deference, the reviewing judge must feel your client did not receive the correct result.

You want your statement of the facts to highlight the injustice.

It is much easier if the facts of your case weigh in favor of the result you are looking to achieve for your client. If your client does not have a favorable equitable position, then you must review the record for issues in his or her favor and underscore those principles within your brief.

But keep in mind what *success* is for your client. For example, how does a potential change in the judgment affect the children involved? How does an appeal impact the finances of your client? Would a victory resulting in a remand, which would mean additional costs for your client, in the long-term outweigh the price of your client's appellate victory?

The results of all outcomes must be considered with your client prior to filing any appeal.

L. OUTCOME

The potential answer to what an appeal's outcome may be requires an in-depth knowledge of both the facts at hand and the legal principles presented. An answer may not be possible until you have fully examined the record, researched all issues, and written your final brief. Even then, you are never entirely certain, as an appeal can sometimes end up in a result you never anticipated.

Appellate courts sometimes find value in an issue you considered only minor. But regardless of where you may end up, it is possible during your review of the record to find significant legal errors providing keys to a reversal or a remand.

M. DISCUSS ALL POSSIBLE OUTCOMES

It is important to be candid with a potential client. There are a number of possible results of a family law appeal. First, inform your client most appeals end up with the appellate court affirming the results from the trial court. After you have had this difficult conversation, explore the possibilities of remand, reversal, and an affirmance of the trial decision, all within the context of winning and losing.

N. REMAND

An appellate court can make a wide variety of decisions that may not result in the end of the case. One possible outcome is the matter being remanded back to the trial court with instructions for further review. This often happens when an appellate court finds a legal error but then requires the trial court to reconsider its original rulings in light of the appellate decision.

PRACTICE POINTER

Always inform your client that an appeal does not always end with a simple win or lose.

O. LOSING

You must consider what may happen if the judgment is affirmed and the appeal lost. Consider the reality of losing an appeal. How will the loss affect your client? Will the risk of losing the appeal cause further harm to the client? To the children? Does closure *now* make sense for both the client and the issues?

P. TO NOT APPEAL

Why not file an appeal of a family law decision?

A client's immediate reaction to an adverse ruling is likely to seek further justice in a higher court. However, your same client wanting to pursue an appeal is unlikely to understand the significant expense, time, and odds against the success of an appeal.

In addition, your client is unlikely to understand how an appeal may affect the current orders or judgment issued by the lower court.

For example, a client who seeks a reduction in child support may not realize he must continue to pay child support at the same level during the pendency of an appeal.

Once you educate a client on the harsh realities of an appeal, the desire to seek further justice can wane.

In addition, unlike other areas of civil law, family law judgments are usually not stayed pending an appeal.

The house may be sold, for example, thereby losing the purpose of the appeal itself. You may win the battle but still end up losing the war.

A stay may involve a supersedeas bond. These bonds are prohibitively expensive, as they often include the amount in dispute, interest, and an estimate of costs and fees that may ultimately be awarded.

Q. MEDIATION PROGRAMS

Both sides face risks and delays when an appeal is taken by a party or both parties. There are multiple points when mediation is an alternative. A well-drafted docketing statement or an appellant's brief might alter the appellee's opinion on whether sticking to the lower court's judgment is wise.

Many states offer appellate court mediation programs.

You may find these programs to be useful, if available in your local jurisdiction. They may help you settle a case without involving the appellate court panel and reduce costs for the courts and your clients. It is an option to explore with your client.

R. SETTLEMENT

Discuss with your client whether it is possible to settle the matter short of filing an appeal. The client, or the opposing side, may be loath to settle after a favorable judgment, but it must be considered with your client, particularly in the context of whether it makes sense to go forward with an appeal.

In general, any recommendation to settle is usually not possible until you have reviewed the record and researched any legal issues presented. At a minimum, conduct a full and careful review of the record before exploring settlement options with your client. Look at the facts as they are in the record and not just your client's or trial counsel's memory. Consider the standard of review. Then make your settlement recommendation.

You may consider an initial engagement *to review the matter only* and have the client execute a fee agreement clearly defining the limited nature of your representation.

After your review is completed, all options can be discussed with your client and a new engagement can be executed.

S. SETTLEMENT AFTER THE APPEAL IS DOCKETED

The timing of any settlement is often unpredictable. There are times the mere filing of a notice of appeal followed by the appeal being docketed in the appellate court may move your client, or an opposing party, to settle the matter.

If you come to an agreement, after the matter is within jurisdiction of the appellate court, then an appropriate joint motion is filed with the appellate court to dismiss the appeal.

Once the appeal is dismissed by the appellate court, then the settlement can be effectuated in the trial court.

T. CONCLUSION

In summary, the decision to appeal is carefully weighed with each client and in each case. All possible alternatives are discussed, including post-trial motions and possible future modifications within the lower court. Thereafter, the possible outcomes of an appeal are discussed with your client, including the long odds against winning and the substantial costs and risks of losing the appeal and the potential for remand. After you have had these discussions with your client, then it is time to ask yourself a few ethical questions (discussed in Chapter 2) before choosing to appeal.

Ethical Considerations 2

A. ATTORNEY/CLIENT RELATIONSHIP

Family law appeals are unique and challenging. The process involves a significant commitment of your time, thought, effort, and energy. And more importantly, it involves a significant amount of your potential client's emotions, someone who may be outraged at the judge's decision. Thus any appeal is extremely important to your highly sensitive client, and the level of difficulty presented for you is on the extreme end of the practice of law.

The relationship between you and your client is an important consideration. An appeal is more productive—regardless of outcome—when there is a match between you and your client. There are a number of things to consider for an appeal, but consider whether you want to appeal a decision *for that particular client.*

First, consider whether you can work with your client in an open, direct, and honest manner. Clients in family law appeals are generally emotional, angry, and seeking a sense of justice with a mix of flat-out revenge. They come to you feeling wronged by a former spouse and by the system.

You are the last stop in an emotional and costly period of his or her life. You have to recognize the perspective he or she brings in the door, and then determine if you can have a successful partnership.

Prior to committing to a case, be mindful of what is best for both you and your potential client. Consider asking the following threshold questions that will help determine if you are the appropriate fit with the client to take the case to the appeals court.

B. EXPECTATIONS

What does your potential client hope to accomplish by pursuing an appeal? Is this a person you can work with? Which side will you represent in the appeal? Will you be representing the appellant? Is it likely you need to write both an appellant and a reply brief? Or will you be representing the appellee and need to write only one brief?

What about the potential for oral argument? Is oral argument allowed in your locality? Is it likely to be ordered if it is permissible? Will you need to request it? What will you need to do to prepare for an oral argument?

Does the potential client have realistic expectations of all possible outcomes? Are you comfortable advocating on behalf of your client under the circumstances involved? Do you agree with the goal of your client?

Do not be afraid to ask your potential client all of these questions prior to committing to the engagement of the appeal.

C. THE RECORD

Consider the trial court record to assess your potential client.

Do you have full access to all the material and people you need to assess the case? How was the record handled by the court? Did your client have trial counsel who made all appropriate objections to preserve the record for a potential appeal?

Was the client pro se?

Does the fact your client was pro se affect the preservation of the record? What evidence was introduced at trial? Where is it now?

Is the record complete? And most critically, will the record that was created enable you to file an appropriate appeal?

Often this review may be bereft of transcripts, and transcripts may not be available before the deadline to take appeal. So the client needs to be aware of the costs of transcripts and that the review is incomplete without a full record.

D. UNIQUE QUESTIONS

Ask the following questions of all potential family law appellate clients:

Is your client simply motivated by revenge?
Are they simply trying to inflict further emotional or financial harm upon a former spouse?
Does he or she have a clear goal?
Is there a reasonable chance of success?

All of these questions must be answered by your client and then weighed against the myriad possibilities of the outcome of an appeal.

PRACTICE POINTER

Never take an appeal when a client does not have a clear goal to achieve from the appeals court.

If you are not satisfied with your potential client's answers, then decline the representation. There are other cases and other clients.

Consider referring the client to a different attorney if there is anything about the case that has potential but the client is not the right fit for you or your firm.

After a long and bitter trial, you may find that you are "just out of gas" with this case. Some cases require a fresh, new perspective.

When that happens, it is helpful for both client and attorney to obtain new counsel with someone who may bring objectivity and new, fresh ideas to the matter. So do not be afraid to refer the case to new counsel. It is just good practice.

In the end, always trust your instincts before you take on a client's appeal.

E. BE REALISTIC

Be both clear and realistic with your client about the challenges of an appeal and the statistical chance against prevailing.

Always ask point-blank: What do you want to achieve here? What is the best possible result of an appeal? What is an acceptable result? What if we lose again? Are you willing to explore settlement?

You must assess if your client's goals are realistic.

Does the possible appeal stand a chance in the face of the broad discretion granted probate court judges in family courts? Many times, the answer is that the client's goal is unrealistic or unreasonable.

F. TIME

A potential appellate client needs to understand both the significant amount of time an appeal may take and the significant financial costs to be incurred.

It takes time to review the record, conduct research, and write the briefs. And all this time is spent prior to submission to the reviewing court.

An appeal of a family court judgment to an appellate court often takes a year or longer. The time involved and the uncertainty in result is not for each client.

It is possible your client, after months of slugging it out with a spouse in the lower court and spending thousands of dollars, may not have the desire to continue the fight.

For example, perhaps the matter involves a long and protracted child custody matter. There are times when closure might be worth more than the time, cost, and toll of an appeal.

Encourage your client to conduct his or her own cost-benefit analysis of pursuing an appeal and explore all other potential options, including resolution.

Regardless of the client's decision, ensure prior to undertaking the appeal that the potential client is fully informed about the time considerations and the significant costs.

G. OTHER CONSIDERATIONS

If the case involves the division of a marital interest in an ongoing business, understand the effect continued litigation may have upon its operation. The potential for bonding a judgment during the pendency of an appeal may need to be explored.

The potential for interest costs upon a monetary judgment during an appeal is reviewed with your client.

Explore with your client the potential for seeking any post-trial relief with the trial judge prior to pursuing an appeal. This might be a more cost-effective option.

Discuss with your client the option of pursuing the matter in a potential future modification action rather than an appeal.

Sometimes it is better to live to fight another battle than to die on your sword.

H. NEW RETAINERS

Prepare a new and separate fee agreement to be signed by both you and the client before undertaking the appeal. Inform your client the matter is a new action, which requires a new formal written agreement. Ensure the client understands that an appeal is separate and different from your prior agreement. A reminder to always check your local rules for fee agreement requirements and rules pertaining to the charging of legal fees and costs.

Your fee agreement should clearly explain all material terms of your engagement with the client.

Include the exact purpose and limits of your representation. For example, "The representation is limited to the filing of an appeal and ends upon the appellate court issuing a decision."

In the event the matter is remanded, obtain a new executed fee agreement from your client.

Your agreement contains how you charge costs to your client. For example, the hourly rate for legal services performed by my firm is as follows:

Zeus: $500 per hour
Majestic Princess: $350 per hour
Medusa: $250 per hour
Lowly Associate: $200 per hour

An explanation of how these charges are billed is included within your fee agreement or letter of representation:

> This hourly time charge for legal services will include, but is not limited to, receipt and review of file materials, negotiation and conferences, telephone calls, office memoranda, correspondence, legal research, drafting of pleadings or instruments, discovery including depositions, preparation for hearings and trial-court appearances, extraordinary travel and all other appropriate and reasonable activity which is directed toward achieving a favorable result for you.

Allow your client an opportunity to ask any questions about the fee agreement. Suggest he or she obtain additional guidance from another attorney prior to your agreement for representation.

I. FEE AGREEMENTS

Fee agreements are governed by local ethical rules.

Many states impose additional requirements to be covered within your letter of representation or fee agreement. Texas, for example, requires the following:

> On November 7, 1989, the Texas Supreme Court adopted the Texas Lawyer's Creed—a Mandate for Professionalism. Paragraph II, subparagraph 1 of the Creed requires me to advise you of its contents when I undertake representation. A copy of the Creed is enclosed. I believe that I have abided and will continue to abide by the Creed.[11]

11. Appellate Practice in Federal and State Courts § 1.01.

Here is a complete fee agreement example:

Fees are established through the exercise of judgment on each individual matter after considering a number of factors, including the time and labor required, the novelty and difficulty of the issues involved, the skill required to perform the legal services properly, time limitations imposed by the client or by the circumstances, my experience, reputation and ability, the issues involved and the results obtained through our services, the likelihood that such employment will preclude other employment, and the fee customarily charged in the locality by others for similar services.

Generally, our objective of charging a reasonable fee for our services is achieved through maintaining accurate records as to the time spent and then billing for that time in accordance with hourly rates which are established based upon our experience and levels of expertise. Fees derived from these calculations may be modified, taking into consideration any of the other factors involved that are discussed above.

My hourly rate is $______. My associate's rate is $______ an hour, and our paralegal's rate is $____ an hour. These rates are periodically reviewed and are subject to occasional modest adjustments without notice based upon increasing experience and various economic factors, including inflation.

It is our practice to bill on a monthly basis, and payment of my statement is expected within thirty days (30) of receipt of the bill.

In addition to reflecting the charges for our time and expertise, the statements will include costs incurred in the rendition of services, including the actual cost of any outside photocopying expenses, the cost of computerized legal and other research systems, any messenger and special delivery services, any necessary travel expenses, unusual phone expenses, and any extraordinary items, which may be generated by the particular demands of the project involved. These expenses will be owed by you and must be paid within thirty (30) days of billing. Generally, this firm does not bill for sending or receiving faxes or routine telephone expense.

It is our understanding that you will order the record, and we would like a hard copy and an electronic copy of that sent to ________.

> Further, if certain unusual expenses for such things as depositions, witness fees, transcripts, or any other extraordinary expenses are incurred on your behalf, these invoices may be sent directly to you for payment. If experts or consultants are retained or if other third-party support services are required, these individuals or firms will be retained based upon your consent. You will be directly responsible for paying the fees of these individuals or firms and such payments should be made within thirty (30) days of receipt of their invoices. We anticipate that your trial counsel will be handling all of these matters, and that this firm will not be involved in these aspects of your litigation.
>
> You and trial counsel will order the complete transcript of the trial and any other proceedings before the court and make the requisite financial arrangements with the court reporter. Expenses associated with acquiring and copying the transcript, as with the other expenses outlined above, are owed by you without regard to our fee.
>
> If you ever have a question about our billing procedures or statements, please ask me.
>
> It is my policy to require a retainer. In this case, the required retainer is $______. It will be deposited in a trust account. Please provide me with a signed original of this engagement letter, and your tax identification number. I will draw against this retainer to satisfy my monthly statements, copies of which will be sent to you for your information. Once the retainer has dropped below $______, you agree to pay any outstanding balance and replenish the retainer within fourteen (14) days of our invoice requesting that you do so. We will not enter an appearance or begin to read the record until the retainer is deposited and this engagement letter is signed and returned.
>
> Please note that any retainer is not meant to be an estimate of the total fees and expenses to be incurred, but rather, it is your good faith deposit against a portion of such fees and expenses that may be incurred.[12]

It is helpful to put in writing the realities of the statistical likelihood of obtaining a reversal on appeal. Something like the following might be helpful:

---

12. *Id.*

> Actual fees and expenses incurred are a result of many conditions, a number of which are beyond my control, particularly when other parties and multiple lawyers are involved. Accordingly it is important that you understand that I cannot tell in advance how much time a case will take or how much it will cost. It is not unusual for the total cost of appeals in which we are involved to exceed $________.
>
> As you know, we cannot make representations to you as to the probability of ultimate success in your matter, and similarly we cannot guarantee any particular result. The Fifth Circuit Court of Appeals only reverses approximately 10% of the cases that are appealed to it. However, we do agree to exert in good faith our best ethical and professional efforts on your behalf and to keep you informed at each stage of the process.[13]

J. TERMINATION

Your fee agreement contains the terms to terminate your representation with your client; for example, because of nonpayment from a client or a breakdown in communication with your client.

Any termination clause must comply with your ethical responsibilities and local rules. Include how the client may discharge you from service. Take the following example:

> You may terminate our employment at any time by notifying me in writing. Subject to compliance with applicable ethical considerations, we may withdraw from representation in this matter under certain circumstances by notifying you in writing. These circumstances include but are not limited to: if we have good cause for termination; if our withdrawal may be accomplished without a material adverse effect to your interests; or if you fail substantially to fulfill an obligation to us, including the obligation to pay our retainer, or our fees and expenses within thirty (30) days of billing, as agreed. We also reserve the right to terminate our employment if it becomes clear that the appeal is frivolous. Should that happen, we will inform you immediately

13. *Id.*

> and discuss how we should proceed. Upon termination by either party, you will be obligated to pay only for the services rendered and expenses incurred as of the date of receipt of the letter of termination, and any unused portion of the retainer will be refunded to you.[14]

K. INVOLVING THE CLIENT AND TRIAL COUNSEL

Both your client and trial counsel can contribute to your appeal on behalf of your client. With your client's permission first, always sit down with trial counsel and ask a number of pertinent questions about the trial and the judgment of the lower court. Trial counsel may be a great resource for further appellate referrals. Protect your collaborative efforts with trial counsel and assure them you are not there to poach their client from future work, nor are you there to blame them for any error.

Ask trial counsel, What went wrong at trial? Why do you believe the client lost? What did the judge focus upon at trial? What particular facts did the judge rely upon? Was the judge's use of the facts consistent with the application of the proper legal standards? Why should the outcome of the appeal be any different? What is trial counsel's "gut feeling" regarding the result?

You may be surprised, but clients often have good insights on what occurred at trial, which resulted in a judgment not in his or her favor.

Do not disregard client feedback as you prepare to investigate the possibility of an appeal. It is his or her case and he or she has been intimately involved from the beginning, so use him as a valuable resource.

PRACTICE POINTER

Always trust but verify what your client and/or trial counsel state appears in the record.

---

14. *Id.*

Similarly, trial counsel may offer you valuable insights from the experience of being on the "front lines" of the case in the lower court.

One note, however, of caution.

Many times, trial counsel, and your client, may remember events and facts differently from what actually appears in the record. You can find only the pertinent information is missing from the record after you conduct your own review.

Anyone who has reviewed a few transcripts of hearings knows how it can be very different from how it reads later.

For example, a client may tell you a judge said at pretrial, "I would not have to give her the vacation home." Of course, the pretrial discussion is not part of the trial record and the judge's comment is not going to help the client's appeal.

There is only one official record. What is not there does not exist in the realm of appellate practice.

L. BE PREPARED TO ALLOW TRIAL COUNSEL TO READ YOUR DRAFT BRIEF

Allow trial counsel to read any drafts of the brief, but only if your client deems it is appropriate and provides you first with written permission.

Likewise, you may want the client to read a draft brief as well.

Discuss comments with your client and trial counsel to ensure you are covering all pertinent issues in your brief. Consider a reading by another appellate attorney. In complex cases, peer review is very appropriate and protects the client's case.

However, it is *your brief*.

Do not feel compelled to include either trial counsel's thoughts or your client's. Clients are emotional. As a result, they tend to focus on emotional aspects of the record that may not help the appeal.

For example, the wife may testify that her husband—your client—never watched the children, which he protests is false, when you are appealing a property division and not an award of child custody.

PRACTICE POINTER

Do not forget the essential goal of any brief is to persuade the appellate court of your theory as to how the lower court made an error and by doing that, and only that, will it ultimately please your client.

M. ABA MODEL RULES OF PROFESSIONAL CONDUCT

The ABA Model Rules of Professional Conduct and state and federal court rules provide thresholds for proceeding with any appeal. All U.S. states have adopted the Model Rules either in whole or in part.

Always familiarize yourself with the rules of your local jurisdiction and any rules specific in the appellate court that will hear the appeal. Review these ethical rules prior to engaging a client for an appeal in every appeal you are considering.

Here are some of the pertinent rules to consider prior to your engagement of a potential client.

MODEL RULE 3.1 "Meritorious Claims and Contentions"

ABA Model Rule of Professional Conduct 3.1 provides: "A lawyer shall not bring or defend a proceeding, or assert or controvert an issue therein, unless there is a basis in law and fact for doing so that is not frivolous, which includes a good faith argument for an extension, modification or reversal of existing law. . . ." Always avoid filing a frivolous appeal, as it could subject you to discipline for violating your local rules.

In addition, you run the risk of costing your client fees, if your jurisdiction allows for an award against a party who has brought a frivolous appeal. This is an important rule to keep in mind, as many clients are blinded by pure emotion and may convince you to bring an appeal holding little merit. Or you may find yourself responding to such a bad faith appeal.

You have an obligation to "not knowingly . . . fail to disclose to the tribunal legal authority in the controlling jurisdiction known to the lawyer to be directly adverse to the position of the client and not disclosed by opposing counsel." Assess whether there is legal authority directly controlling the outcome of the appeal that is against your client.

MODEL RULE 1.2 "Scope of Representation and Allocation of Authority between Client and Lawyer"

ABA Model Rules of Professional Conduct 1.2(a) provides "a lawyer shall abide by a client's decisions concerning the objectives of representation and, as required by Rule 1.4, shall consult with the client as to the means by which they are to be pursued. A lawyer may take such action on behalf of the client as is impliedly authorized to carry out the representation. A lawyer shall abide by a client's decision whether to settle a matter. . . ."

Ensure you are able to abide by this provision, which highlights the importance of sharing your client's goals in bringing forth the appeal.

MODEL RULE 1.4 "Communications"

ABA Model Rule of Professional Conduct 1.4(a) provides "A lawyer shall: (1) promptly inform the client of any decision or circumstance with respect to which the client's informed consent, as defined in Rule 1.0(e), is required by these Rules; (2) reasonably consult with the client about the means by which the client's objectives are to be accomplished; (3) keep the client reasonably informed about the status of the matter; (4) promptly comply with reasonable requests for information; and (5) consult with the client about any relevant limitation on the lawyer's conduct when the lawyer knows that the client expects assistance not permitted by the Rules of Professional Conduct or other law." Rule 1.4(b) reads, "A lawyer shall explain a matter to the extent reasonably necessary to permit the client to make informed decisions regarding the representation."

Model Rule 1.4 controls and mandates communications between you and your potential client. It is considered in your initial determination whether to accept the client and proceed with his or her appeal.

Clients in family matters can have unreasonable expectations of what may happen in an appeal. This can result in significant problems that may outweigh any interest you have in accepting the case. Always know, there will be other clients and cases. Choose your appellate cases wisely.

PRACTICE POINTER

All fee agreements must be in writing even if it is not required by your local rules.

N. ALWAYS STAY OBJECTIVE

Focus not only on your client, but also on the *actual* legal issues presented rather than the factual disputes between the warring parties.

Let's face it: You can get caught up in your client's own "upset" and emotions regarding the injustice issued by the lower court. Your client is angry. You are angry. You became a lawyer to "right" those "wrongs" and to find fairness and justice. You may find yourself getting caught up in your client's emotional upset at being on the wrong end of the judge's decision. But these feelings are not the reasons for you to bring forward your client's appeal. Losing in itself is not "an urgent *appeal*."

Focus instead on a thorough and rational analysis of all factors involved and steer clients toward sound reasons for filing an urgent plea to the reviewing court. By doing so, you make a good rational and ethical decision to go forward with your client's appeal, and it shows in the strength of the arguments you ultimately make to the appellate court.

3 Interlocutory Relief: What, How, and When to Challenge Orders Prior to Final Judgment

A fundamental rule of appellate practice is there is only one "final judgment." Under this tenet, appellate courts do not review interlocutory rulings by the lower court until a final judgment is reached by the lower court. Keep in mind one caveat: A final order in family law from a trial court with ongoing jurisdiction can be as elusive as a unicorn.

A decision is considered "final" when the litigation is complete. Think when there is nothing further for the trial court to do except implement the judgment.

If an appeal is from a nonfinal order, the appellate court lacks the jurisdiction to hear the matter. The purpose of the rule is to avoid the chaos of multiple appeals while the matter remains within the lower court. If not for this rule, the trial court and the appellate court would be a never ending escalator constantly going up and down.

Notwithstanding the general rule of the lack of appellate relief during the pendency of a matter, states have enacted a framework to seek interlocutory relief.

An important tool in your appellate toolbox is to understand when to seek interlocutory relief. Be familiar with your local rules to understand when and how it is appropriate to challenge the lower court during the pendency of any matter.

PRACTICE POINTER

Apply the same procedure for considering an appeal of a final judgment to take an interlocutory appeal.

A. EXTRAORDINARY WRITS

Asking an appeals court to issue an extraordinary writ is the carrying out of a court's original jurisdiction. Your request is for the reviewing court to apply its vast equitable powers to your client's pending matter.

In substance, a writ petition requests an appeals court to direct a lower court to do something or to refrain from taking some improper action. This is asking the appellate for *extraordinary relief* indeed and is only available in very limited and rare circumstances.

Some courts refer to the jurisdiction to issue writs as its "supervisory" jurisdiction. It is the power of appellate courts to confine inferior tribunals.

Think of it as the Major League Baseball commissioner's office overseeing the umpire crews.

Traditionally, writ review was sought for an order not appealable. But writ relief should not be used as a substitute for an appeal. A writ does not replace an error, which should have been presented as and on an appeal.

Unlike an appeal, which is heard as a matter of right, relief by means of writ is deemed extraordinary, equitable, and entirely discretionary. Therefore, even if a trial court ruling is erroneous, the appellate court is not required to grant an immediate writ petition.

It may instead permit review of the issue to wait on an appeal from the final judgment. As a result, the majority of writ petitions are summarily denied. Hence, extraordinary writs play a small but still vital part of appellate practice.

Let's turn to the family law context.

For example, take a child removal action, where the opposing party receives a favorable temporary order from the trial court allowing relocation of your client's child out of state during the pendency of the action.

What do you do to prevent the move?

To prevent the move during the pendency of the action and prior to a final judgment, a writ stopping the move is necessary from the appellate court.

PRACTICE POINTER

Always proceed with extreme caution in determining whether to challenge an order by interlocutory relief, as the relief you seek is extraordinary.

Most jurisdictions authorize interlocutory orders to be appealed directly to the appellate court. For example, New York allows appeals as of right from an interlocutory order involving parts of the merits or if the order affects a substantial right.[15] This is a very broad-based appellate review for almost any ruling issued by the trial court.

However, the majority of states adhere more closely to the final judgment rule. States do recognize a limited number of judicial exceptions for relief by writ to a higher court.

To qualify for writ relief, demonstrate your client lacks a speedy and adequate remedy at law. Emphasize that a failure to grant your client relief will cause irreparable harm.

Traditional writs are those existing at common law. These writs include mandamus, prohibition, certiorari, and habeas corpus.

B. MANDAMUS

A writ of mandamus (think mandate) is a command from a higher court to a lower court to perform a specific act. Where you are arguing the lower court abused judicial discretion, mandamus is only

15. New York Article 78.

appropriate where you can demonstrate the abuse is extreme and warrants immediate relief from the higher court.

For example, a trial judge improperly dismisses a custodial action under the Uniform Child Custody Jurisdiction and Enforcement Act (UCCJEA). A writ of mandamus is an appropriate means to require the trial court to comply with jurisdictional requirements.

C. PROHIBITION

A writ of prohibition is issued to restrain a threatened judicial act beyond the jurisdiction of the inferior court. This form of writ is employed to restrain the exercise of any unauthorized power by the lower court.

Back to our UCCJEA example discussed above. Let's now suppose a trial judge improperly takes jurisdiction under the UCCJEA. A writ of prohibition would lie where, in this example, the trial court acted without jurisdiction.

D. WRIT OF CERTIORARI—CHILD CUSTODY

The common law writ of certiorari operates to correct a completed nonappealable judicial act in excess of allowable jurisdiction of the trial court. It is distinguishable from the discretionary writ of certiorari issued by the U.S. Supreme Court and other state supreme courts. Those writs are considered statutory in nature.

The common law writ commands the lower court to certify its record to the reviewing court so the higher court may assess whether the lower court acted without proper jurisdiction in its order.

Similar to prohibition, certiorari is available only to redress jurisdictional errors, but the term encompasses any action exceeding the lower court's power to act in an allowable fashion.

For example, suppose a trial court grants a husband's motion to dismiss a child custody portion of his wife's divorce complaint *only*. A writ for certiorari is warranted because the trial court departed from an essential requirement of a divorce action: A child custody count is heard within the divorce proceedings.

The writ of habeas corpus was originally limited to cases of restraint made under claims under color of law. Over time, it has been extended to controversies regarding the custody of children.

E. WRITS—CHILD CUSTODY

When you have a child custody action involved, the habeas action takes on the nature of an equitable proceeding. The trial judge's duty is to act within the best interest of the child. This can result in the rights of the parents being subordinated to those of the child.

Habeas proceedings, which require prompt judicial action, are intended to affect a prompt return of a child to the person entitled to custody. They are not designed to adjudicate the merits of the underlying custody dispute between the warring parents over custody of the child.

The Hague Convention and the International Child Abduction Remedies Act, which looks only to whether a child is wrongfully retained from his or her habitual residence, is a good example of this form of writ.

In fact, actions under the Hague Convention to return a child to the habitual home are handled in practice by courts as petitions for writs of habeas corpus.

A Hague action requires the court to expedite the matter, and these cases are required to move swiftly whether filed within the state or federal court. Both options are available to your client.

An appeal under the Hague Convention is subject to expedited treatment of Hague matters within the lower court.

F. STATUTORY WRITS

All jurisdictions have specific statutes authorizing the review of specific orders by writ petition. These *statutory writs* are exactly what they seem. The statute provides the authorization to the appeals court for review.

The critical difference between traditional and statutory writs is that traditional writs are subject to equitable deadlines. Thus, an unreasonable delay in seeking the relief *may*, but not always, bar the relief you are seeking for your client. In contrast, the filing deadline for a statutory writ is mandated by statute, so it is often a specific required timeline to be followed.

In California, for example, a ruling on a motion to disqualify a judge is reviewable only by petition for writ of mandate filed within ten days after service of entry of the court's order.[16] The statutory writ is the exclusive avenue for seeking appellate review of the ruling on the motion. As a result, the decision is neither directly appealable nor reviewable in a final judgment appeal.

G. ABOLISHED TRADITIONAL WRITS

A few states "abolished" traditional writs.

Instead, these states enacted more flexible remedies for reviewing orders that traditionally were reviewable by writ at common law. New York, Arizona, Pennsylvania, Tennessee, Vermont, Washington, and Massachusetts permit courts to review interlocutory orders before "final judgment" when it is reasonable under the circumstances.[17]

However, all statutory schemes require the prompt review of certain final orders. For example, actions to terminate a parent's custodial rights require prompt review by an appellate court.

H. QUESTIONS CERTIFIED TO YOUR STATE SUPREME COURT

What if you have an important and novel issue of law at the trial court level requiring a ruling by your state's highest court? For example, a portion of a new alimony statute pertaining to its definition of the word *retirement*, where the statutory definition is unclear.

States have adopted procedural rules to certify a question or to seek an advisory opinion during the pendency of the matter to the

16. Donna Furth, *Seeking Review of Interlocutory Orders: By Appeal or Writ*, 34 ABA Family Advocate, no. 4, 2014.

17. *Id.*

state's highest court. These limited issues of review of an interlocutory matter are rare circumstances. They are similar to the extraordinary writs discussed above, as you are asking a court to rule on a matter still pending within the trial court.

I. SINGLE JUSTICE PRACTICE

In Massachusetts, single justice practice is a good example of a state's framework for challenging interlocutory orders.[18] The procedure and practice based upon single justice practice in Massachusetts is briefly outlined below as an illustration of expectations and requirements to appeal an interlocutory order.

1. Procedure

Cases are opened upon the filing of one original petition, application, or complaint, together with the requisite filing fee.

You are required in your petition to put forth the following: the lower court's procedural history, including the name of the court and justice; the docket number; the trial date (if applicable); a brief discussion of the order subject to review; and the grounds upon which review is necessary and the relief sought.

The single justice is empowered to handle the petition in a variety of ways. He or she may:

- Decline to act.
- Determine the issue presented.
- Allow the relief requested.
- Allow the relief sought in part and deny it in part.
- Deny the relief sought.
- Transfer the case to a lower court if appropriate.
- Remand the case to the trial court to establish a record or advise the trial court to proceed in a certain manner.

When the single justice is presented with a novel question of law, which is unresolved by the existing case, he or she may choose to report the matter to the full appellate court.

18. Massachusetts Single Justice Practice and Procedure.

Practice Pointer

An interlocutory appeal is not a substitute for an appeal after final judgment.

J. PLEADING AND DISCOVERY MATTERS

Pretrial decisions can substantially impact your client in family law matters. For example, a temporary custody order issued against your client early on in a matter can turn to a permanent judgment down the road against your client. A direct appeal from a critical interlocutory order may prevent irreparable harm to your client. As a result, states do recognize exceptions to the final judgment rule for seeking review of major pretrial orders by either permissive appeal or writ.

K. TEMPORARY ORDERS OF CHILD CUSTODY

Temporary child custody orders were not appealable at common law and are not appealable in most states. However, a few states recognize the impactful nature of initial decisions, which can dictate the ultimate outcome and allow for review by writ. Connecticut is one example.[19]

If a temporary *order is directly appealable*, the failure to not pursue the claim at the earliest time can waive the issue from an appeal of the final judgment. Therefore, it is imperative to understand your local rules regarding the finality of temporary orders and their effect upon appellate rights.

A few states permit discretionary appeals in child custody matters from nonfinal orders. For example, in Illinois, a party may petition for leave to appeal from child custody–related interlocutory orders even when seeking such an appeal is not found within the rules of the court. And the state of Maryland recognizes an exception to the final judgment rule permitting interlocutory appeals from orders, which deprive a parent of his or her custodial rights.

19. *Id.*

Indeed, all states have enacted statutory arrangements designed to protect children from abuse and neglect. Immediate appeals from interlocutory orders protecting children is universally permissible.

Regardless of the local framework, it is imperative for you to assess whether to appeal an interlocutory order when it involves issues related to child custody. Be familiar with your applicable local statutes and rules of court. If no immediate appeal is available, consider whether a writ review could be sought in your case.

For example, in Texas and Alabama, relief is granted by writ of mandamus. While in Arizona (a state that abolished common law writs), relief is granted by statutory authorization, called "special action."

An Arizona case, under "special action," illustrates the critical role writs can play.[20] The petitioner, a seventeen-year-old child of the battling parties, sought to intervene in his custody dispute between his parents.

The child filed a motion to intervene as a party and then a motion to appear by retained counsel. The inferior court denied his motions, which were opposed by his own parents, who seemingly finally agreed on something.

The Arizona Court of Appeals granted the "special action" jurisdiction and found the child was an interested party in the matter and the lower court abused its discretion by failing to appoint him counsel.

Writs possess the ability to provide extraordinary relief to your client, and in some circumstances, relief is afforded when it is otherwise unavailable for your client.

Child custody temporary orders issued during the pendency of a matter are essential and often become permanent custody orders. There is an immediate desire to seek further relief when temporary custodial orders go against your client.

It is important to carefully evaluate whether—depending upon local rules, the law, and the facts involved—it is practical to seek further relief at the early stages of the game.

---

20. J.A.R. v. Superior Court, 877 P.2d 1323 (Ariz. Ct. App. 1994).

L. THE TYPE OF TEMPORARY ORDER TO CHALLENGE

The following child custody order illustrates an order to challenge prior to a final judgment. Suppose the standard for temporary orders in your jurisdiction is the following:

> A change in custody during the pendency of a complaint for modification of a prior custody order must be based on "*specific findings of fact* . . . which clearly demonstrate the injury, harm or damage that might reasonably be expected to occur if relief pending a judgment of modification is not granted."
>
> These specific findings are necessary and required during the pendency of a modification action and cannot be ignored by the court.

But what if the lower court did not enter the required written specific findings to justify its order to modify the parenting plan of the parties, by temporary order, during a modification action?

For example, the order states *only the following*:

> The Father shall have sole physical custody with no further parenting time for Mother.

In this example, the lower court committed a clear error of law requiring reversal, as the lower court did not enter specific findings of fact demonstrating harm or injury necessary to change the parties' agreed-upon parenting plan in conformity with the statute. The court's order here changing physical custody without specific findings explaining why there was a change is custody must be reversed since it does not meet the minimum requirements of the statute.

M. CONCLUSION

When a lower court commits a plain and reversible error of law and there is interlocutory relief available, then challenge the decision with the reviewing court. Any time the lower court does not follow a statutory mandate, then action must be considered. When the law is clearly in favor of your client, then employ your local rules to take the appropriate action and seek interlocutory relief.

4 Creating, Protecting, and Reviewing the Record

A. CREATING THE RECORD

You must put forward your best possible case before the trial court on every one of your client's issues rather than relying on changing a judgment by an appeal. The odds of winning an appeal are against your client.

Many courts of appeal publish statistics; even the rawest of data, such as total appeals filed over the total sustained, would be a very chilling and informative piece of information to share with potential clients. Thus, the best chance to prevail is always with the trial judge.

Ensure you are thorough in your presentation of evidence. Make all timely objections. And keep an eye on creating an excellent record to protect the possibility of an appeal.

Practice Pointer

When in doubt, always object to preserve the record.

The best way to protect the record is to do the following at trial:

1. Make all timely objections.
2. Properly admit both testimony and evidence.
3. When the trial judge rules evidence is inadmissible, stand up and make an offer of proof.

If the record is not protected, appellate courts presume there is no error in the judgment to correct.

The governing principle of creation of the record is if an issue is not clearly reflected within the physical confines of the case file found within the lower court, it is not considered in appellate review.

Appellate courts require that the record be demonstrative on any issue up for further consideration.

Timely objections must be made, offers of proof must be presented, and properly filed motions and objections to improper evidence must exist within the trial court record.

Evidence must be offered. Trial exhibits must be introduced. The record must be created for appellate review of any issue.

B. PROTECT THE RECORD

It is your job to both create and protect the record. This is best accomplished by raising an issue of law in writing with the trial court. This gives a chance to explain your legal reasoning both to the trial judge and to any reviewing court in the future. It saves time in the future when you develop the issue further for a reviewing court. Cite to the statute, rule, or legal precedent that supports the argument you are making to the court.

When you are able to address issues in writing, it gives the appellate court the opportunity to look at what you wrote, the opposition, and the lower court's ruling on the matter.

For example, after divorce, the wife wishes to relocate with a minor child to a new state over five hundred miles away. She files a subsequent removal action complaint along with a motion to relocate the child during the pendency of the action.

Though there may be legitimate factual reasons for the move, there may be constitutional or statutory issues about interstate travel or custodial rights as basis for an objection to the relocation. To protect the record, raise all those objections at the motion hearing.

Practice Pointer

A written argument is better than an oral argument to protect the record.

The next best practice to a written pleading is to make your arguments orally with the trial judge so your position is clearly articulated and presented within the record.

The goal of the oral argument is to be as clear and detailed as you can. Orally raise the statute, rule, or legal precedent in court as if it is in writing. Think to yourself whatever you say is magnified by the spotlight of the appellate court review of the record.

Practice Pointer

If you make an oral argument, and if time allows it, write it down to ensure all your points make it into the record.

C. PRETRIAL PROCEEDINGS

Create your record from the very beginning of the matter.

Be very conscious of preserving issues from the start of your case, including any possible trial issues. Of course, be aware that it is not always possible to raise every issue within the record. But at the same time, keep in mind that the consequences of failing to preserve an issue at trial is that the issue is waived for an appeal.

When you are diligent in your record creation from the start of the action, you create a more thorough and complete record of any possible issue.

Begin record protection with your very first filings, including the complaint and any answer or counterclaim. For example, states require clients to establish claims for any relief in the initial papers filed with the court.

In South Carolina, the parties must request alimony in either their complaint for divorce or their answer to the complaint for divorce. Likewise, in North Carolina, you must lay out in the complaint a "sufficient basis" to give a spouse a "fair notice of the grounds" for an alimony claim or risk being denied the alimony requested.

Although there are exceptions to pleading rules and family law courts apply equity principals when compliance with rules are less than perfect, it is not worth chancing whether an appellate court will be as accommodating with your client's appeal.

D. PENDENTE LITE MOTIONS

"Pendente lite" motions or "temporary order" motions are fertile ground for appellate issues. These orders are important for preserving and/or potentially waiving issues in the record by not bringing them forth during the early stages of an action. Understand how your local rules review the issuance of the trial court's temporary orders, so if necessary, you can take immediate action.

Actions can include:

1. File an interlocutory appeal.
2. Raise any necessary objections to preserve an appellate argument for a later appeal.
3. Advise your client when there are no available appellate options at the present time after denial of an order during the early days of the litigation.

E. FINANCIAL STATEMENTS

All states require each party to submit a financial affidavit listing all income and expenses and all assets and liabilities under the pains and penalties of perjury. These financial statements, which are often submitted to the trial court during early stages of litigation, may contain errors. Errors found within financial statements can be very costly to your client.

Consider the following example.

Your client, Roberta, overvalues a rare and valuable painting on her financial affidavit by $250,000. She claims a value of $500,000 rather than the actual appraised value by a certified appraiser of $250,000.

Similarly, your party opponent, Malcolm, neglects in his financial statement a business debt of $250,000. Some states prevent either Roberta or Malcolm from later challenging the financial disclosures submitted to the court.

As a result, it is imperative to protect the record at all stages by ensuring all assets and liabilities are always accurate on all financial affidavits and statements. Emphasize the importance of these "forms" to all your clients each time they are required to make a submission to the court. This is not only good practice but it also allows the record to be properly preserved for an appeal.

PRACTICE POINTER

Add a footnote on all financial statements stating the financial statement is subject to an update for any unintended errors or omissions.

F. TRIAL OBJECTIONS

Be vigilant in raising potential errors to the trial judge. All potential appellate claims need to be adequately preserved. Preservation is both defensive and offensive. You are reacting to your opponent's arguments and to the trial court's rulings, while ensuring the facts and arguments you need in the record are raised.

You must object to exhibits and testimony to preserve the record. If any objection exists, you must say "objection" and ensure your objection is clearly stated and articulated.

Here is the mentality to bring to trial:

"Objection."
"Counsel, you have now objected four times in a row."
"That's correct, Your Honor."
"You do not need to object again."
"Objection."

"Counsel . . ."
"So long as the record is clear, Your Honor."
"You have made yourself quite clear!"

State the specific basis for your objections and list every possible ground for the basis of your objections.

For example, perhaps there is a "hearsay" objection from an out-of-court discussion, but perhaps you also object under "relevancy" grounds. You are not afforded a different basis for the objection in the future. Always strive to be overly thorough in the purpose and reason for your objection.

It may seem simple to make objections during trial. However, in practice, your trial judge may display little patience for all of your objections and all of your arguments.

But your job is to preserve the record and not to always please a judge.

When things get "testy" with the trial judge, attempt the following:

1. Remind the court of your ethical obligation to object to protect and preserve the record.
2. Ask for permission to brief the court on the issue at a later time and to articulate your reasoning for the objection.
3. Always be as polite as possible.
4. Always remain calm in the face of potential judicial annoyance.

In the event the trial judge continues to be obstructive as to your obligation to create the record, then ask the trial judge to indicate on the record why explanatory objections are prohibited. This tactic allows you to point to the record exchange and explain the dilemma you faced in front of the appellate court.

Regardless of any resistance to your vigor in creating the record, be ever vigilant for an opportunity to raise the issue again.

Sometimes, a similar objection can be raised to a different piece of evidence or to witness testimony offered by your party opponent. Do not be afraid to raise the objection yet again.

The preservation of the record requires persistence and some deal of creativity, so try different angles to raise your arguments.

PRACTICE POINTER

Maintain in your trial binder a list of evidentiary objections to cite a specific rule quickly during trial.

The knowledge of local evidentiary rules is critical to creating a *good* record for any possible appeal. For example, states require you to renew an objection to evidence after filing a motion in limine to preclude admission.

Always object again during the trial to the potential inadmissible evidence even when the trial court has denied your motion in limine prior to trial. A failure to renew the objection could destroy your appellate argument or at least force you to waste precious brief space arguing why your claim should still be heard.

G. SIDEBARS OR IN CAMERA CONVERSATIONS

Both sidebars or in camera conversations pose a problem for your ability to properly preserve the record. If a critical discussion occurs outside of the courtroom or even off the record between the judge and counsel, it is likely lost for appellate consideration.

So, what do you do?

It is your job to preserve *on the record* the critical off-record conversations. Consider the following options:

1. Ask your trial judge to restate for the record the conversation off the record, thereby putting it back on the record.
2. Cease the off-the-record discussion to ensure it happens on the record.
3. In the event the trial judge does not allow you to restate it for the record or does not stop the off-the-record discussion, then when you are back on the record, make a statement to ensure there is reference to what transpired off the record. (This may draw the ire of an angry judge, but hey, once again, your job is to always protect the record.)
4. File a written motion or memorandum incorporating the discussion.

H. VERBAL PRESERVATION PRACTICE TIPS

Always focus on the following during trial to create the record:

1. Pay attention to what your opponent is stating.
2. Say something in response when necessary.
3. Be clear in your position.
4. Be direct in your argument.
5. Be specific in your argument.
6. Be expansive, when necessary.
7. Be persistent.

I. THE FACTUAL RECORD

Be conscious of the important threshold in making your case and then build the factual record upon them. Let's take a fault grounds divorce, such as adultery.

PRACTICE POINTER

Create your findings of fact prior to trial, and during trial check them off as you establish each fact.

You need to provide evidence to meet the required elements contained within the statue for adultery. Ensure you introduce evidence to prove the affair. For example, an exhibit of the incriminating e-mail to the husband's paramour and testimony from your client as to her discovery of this piece of evidence. By proving statutory elements, you create your record.

Otherwise, if you fail to build the appropriate record on appeal, you lack the sufficient factual evidence—exhibit and testimony—to argue that the trial court erred in its findings of fact.

PRACTICE POINTER

Use "chalks" to summarize evidence for the trial. But the "chalk" is not evidence per se and the underlying documents and/or exhibits must be submitted into evidence to preserve the record.

J. POST-TRIAL SUBMISSIONS

States permit parties to submit proposed findings of fact and/or proposed orders prior to trial or even after the trial ends. These post-trial submissions are critical to frame your case to the trial judge by summarizing the salient facts and legal arguments for both the trial judge and for any potential appeal. These filings are crucial for preserving issues for appeal and must be treated very carefully.

Family law matters turn upon the critical facts. At every step of the litigation, develop and argue your salient facts. Post-trial submissions are an additional opportunity to clarify and complete the record.

In addition, if you include a certain proposed finding of fact and the trial court adopts the proposition, you could be barred from arguing the finding is erroneous on appeal. In fact, it is not unusual for the appellate court to blame you for "inducing" or "inviting" an error, thereby denying your client relief.

Similarly, if the opposing party files proposed findings or orders, it behooves you to object as necessary or file your own in response. Your failure to act could potentially be deemed a waiver of any objection, if the trial court adopts your opponent's proposed findings. Your protest to your opponent's filings within the appeal courts is unlikely to be successful, as the appellate court deems you waived the issue by not objecting in the trial court.

K. UNDERSTANDING THE RECORD

Not only is it critical to create the record, but also prior to any appeal, you should conduct a thorough review of the record. There is no substitute to understand all aspects of the trial record.

The trial record consists of each and every document filed in the court below and every word said in the presence of the judge. It includes all exhibits at trial.

Different courts have different procedures for compiling the record from the court below. Some courts assemble the record subject to counsel providing and ordering trial transcripts.

Speak to your local clerk to understand the procedure for how the record is assembled by the trial court. Regardless of a court's procedure, appellate rules place the burden of "assembly" on the appellant. Discuss with the clerk how to obtain and/or file the trial transcripts.

PRACTICE POINTER

Have a court stenographer present during a trial if there is a possibility of an appeal.

L. THE REVIEW OF THE RECORD

The first step in reviewing the record is to take a very close look at the judgment, findings of fact, and/or the court-issued rationale. This provides an understanding of not only the end result, but also the connection of application of facts to the law. After you have a pretty good understanding of the salient issues, it is a good idea to obtain the transcripts and review the evidence submitted at trial.

PRACTICE POINTER

Limit your initial representation to a record review in order to determine the validity of an appeal.

Then review the transcripts and the evidence submitted at trial. Review the complete record again. Yes, there just is no substitute for your own review of the entire record.

Depending on the matter and local practice, transcripts may not be available in enough time for them to be reviewed prior to the deadline for filing of the notice of appeal. Or, the costs of those transcripts may be cost prohibitive until the client decides that taking appeal is prudent. Consider whether there is an electronic record. In a recent case in Kansas, the court of appeals found the electronic recordings of court proceedings were subject to Kansas Open records act, and access must be granted.[21]

21. Baker v. Hayden, 55 Kan. App. 2d 473, 419 P.3d 31 (2018).

Personally review the record and limit any delegation to a subordinate. There are too many nuances in an appellate record to be missed by a novice team member. Utilize a junior team members to help organize the record, but always personally review it.

Use detailed notes to form the basis for writing the statement of facts in your brief and to assist in preparing any oral argument. Be sure to flag crucial portions of the record. You can return to those critical trial points for use within your Record Appendix.[22]

Even if you were the trial lawyer, review the actual record. You often remember facts or even trial moments differently from what actually happened. Memories of trial events can play tricks on your mind. A second look prior to proceeding with an appeal is well worth the time spent.

M. IMPORTANCE OF FACTS, JUST THE FACTS

Appeals, like trials, tend to start and end with the facts.

In reviewing the record, look for crucial points, which when included in a statement of facts in your appellate brief motivates the appellate court to look for errors of law supporting a remand or reversal of the judgment. Even as good as you are at trial, you sometimes may miss facts or even legal issues hiding in plain sight that are glaring to experienced appellate counsel.

Identifying winning issues or potential winning facts is the most important part of reviewing the record. Each case turns on its own facts.

Careful attention must be paid to the key facts pertaining to each legal issue.

Or identify authorities to support the appellate court's rulings if an affirmance is your ultimate goal.

But essential to your review and analysis is determining if the potential appellate issues are preserved for your potential appeal and are not waived.

22. Record Appendix (RA). The Record Appendix is capitalized to distinguish your understanding from the record.

N. WHAT TO LOOK FOR

During the review of the record, what errors of fact and/or law are you seeking?

1. Findings of fact inconsistent with evidence *actually* submitted at trial.
2. The judgment seems to be inconsistent with the findings of fact made by the judge.
3. Extreme prejudice on the record toward your client by the judge (unusual, but the more incidents found the better the argument).
4. The judgment appears to be incomprehensible in light of facts or is beyond court authority. (This is the *what the heck* feeling you have when you review the record.)
5. The judge failed to perform her statutory responsibility to consider all required factors under a given statute. (A good example would be a judge delegating to a third party to make a custodial decision without any statutory authority to do so, such as adopting the recommendation of a Guardian ad litem without making an independent judgment.)
6. The potential client is denied constitutional rights, such as due process (for example, a lack of evidentiary hearing on a contempt hearing).
7. The application of the law is clearly erroneous. (Look for a new statute or law.)
8. Some form of judicial abuse of discretion. (You may feel something here that requires further analysis or review.)

These potential errors need to be identified in your review of the record to determine the viability of an appeal. But the fact an error is identified by the trial court is not sole grounds for pursuit of an appeal.

Be mindful the appellate court is there to protect your client's rights but only when a *significant trial court error* is crying out for correction.

O. STANDARDS OF REVIEW (BRIEFLY)

Be familiar with the standards of review an appellate court applies (discussed in more detail in Chapter 5). For now, understand if you represent the appellant, you want the appeals court to apply a strict standard of review. If you represent the appellee, you want a standard applied more generous to the trial judge.

The following standards of review are universal to family law appeals:

1. The trial judge's findings are clearly erroneous.
2. If the findings are not clearly erroneous, then the appellate courts may consider whether the trial judge abused his or her discretion.
3. An appellate court may find an abuse of discretion by a trial judge, if it believes no other reasonable judge could have reached the same conclusion.
4. If there is an error of law, they are reviewed de novo. *De novo* is a fancy term for "new," and the appellate court gives no deference to the trial court's legal rulings. (*Plenary review* is another term used for *de novo*.)
5. Contract interpretation, like enforcement of separation agreements, is reviewed under the de novo standard.

P. THE WELL-WRITTEN RECORD

Be mindful during your review of the record that a well-written trial court opinion is not beneficial for your potential appeal. Such opinions "create [their] own presumption of correctness by the force of [their] reasoning and the quality of [their] examination of law and precedent."[23] The better the quality of the written decision by the trial court, the harder to challenge the decision in the appellate court.

---

23. George A. Somerville, *Standards of Appellate Review,* in APPELLATE PRACTICE MANUAL (Priscilla A. Schwab ed., 1992).

Q. CONCLUSION

In summary, it is your obligation to create a proper trial record for any appeal. The record (if you were not trial counsel) in any event must be sufficient for an appellate court to review your legal claims. Otherwise, your appeal ends before it begins.

When you are trial counsel, file appropriate written arguments and make timely objections. Be vigilant at all times in creating the record even when confronted with a trial judge's resistance.

Creating a record is not always easy when confronted with a single judge for the entirety of the matter—the same judge you see the next morning in a different matter—but it is a critical obligation to create and preserve the record at all times.

Prior to commencing any appeal, a good, thorough review of the record is necessary, even if you were trial counsel. A review of the trial itself highlights the strengths and weaknesses of any appeal to come. An appeal will always begin and end with the record created.

5 Understanding Standards of Appellate Review

Your appellate advocate job is to convince appellate court justices a decision made by the trial court is wrong and also harmful or to support the righteousness of the trial court. Where to begin? The first place to start is the appropriate standard of review.

The concept of standards of review may seem fairly academic, but it is a critical component of appellate practice. A working understanding of appellate review standards is necessary to undertake an appeal for your client. Take the following example:

A party argues at oral argument that the lower court's findings of fact in a child custody issue are clearly erroneous.

"But, Counsel," the appellate court states, "in your brief, you did not argue the trial judge made any erroneous finding of fact."

Standards of review are the shining light applied by appellate courts to decisions of the lower courts. Thus, appellate courts are diligent in identifying and then applying the proper standard of review to a judgment of the trial court.

Think of it as the appeals court's standard of proof.

As a result of the importance of the standard of review, the appeals court requires you to show a similar recognition and application of the correct standard of review in framing your issues and arguments on appeal.

In fact, most appellate courts require you to identify, usually in the argument section of your opening brief, the standard of review applicable to each issue contested on appeal. When you evaluate the merits of taking an appeal, include with your review of the record the potential standard of review to apply to the matter.

The dilemma is appellate courts stringently apply the applicable standard of review when faced with decisions from a trial court on pure legal issues. The problem in family law appeals is they do not tend to center around pure legal issues.

Instead, family law appeals depend heavily upon unique factual situations of the parties. Those "fact-based" decisions are given greater discretion by the reviewing court. The bar is therefore set higher for you. Your job is to utilize the critical facts into the substantive law and then use the appropriate standard of review to convince the appeals court exactly how the lower court got it all wrong.

A. THE STANDARDS

Generally, appellate courts apply differing standards, depending upon:

1. Where the appeals court is asked to review the facts upon which the decision is based.

Or

2. Where the appeals court is asked to review the exercise of discretion by the lower court.

The terms vary from jurisdiction to jurisdiction when describing what is meant by "standards of review," but they are mainly referred to as *substantial competent evidence*, *abuse of discretion*, or *de novo review*. We can place them into five primary categories of standards to be familiar with in making your own arguments.

B. REVIEWING THE LAW

Let's start with a pure *law*-driven standards of review.

C. DE NOVO REVIEW

When an appellate issue involves the interpretation of the law, appellate courts review the issue de novo—that is, "new" or "from the beginning." Think of it as a restart after a false start. Although every judge and every court decides how to apply the law, the question before the court is, "What is the law?" The ultimate decision lies with a higher court. These cases can be a bit rare or unusual in the family law context. This is also referred to as a *plenary review*.

If your case is of first impression or involves an area of unique law, the trial judge may not have the last word. So, plan your trial accordingly with a keen eye on ensuring the record is complete on this novel or new issue. This is where a well-researched trial brief may be indispensable.

Potential appellate clients must understand that just because appellate courts analyze issues of law without deference to the trial judge's conclusion does not mean their potential appeal has a higher likelihood of success. Very often, two independent, impartial decision makers simply reach the same decision.

D. LEGAL SUFFICIENCY OF THE EVIDENCE

The second classification of standards of appellate review is to understand legal sufficiency of the evidence. States use the following terminology in this classification: *traditional legal sufficiency*, *substantial evidence review*, and the *clearly erroneous rule*.

Most states adopt what is considered the traditional legal sufficiency standard of review. The "no evidence" or "legal insufficiency" point challenges the legal ability based upon the evidence submitted at trial to support a particular fact-finding made by the judge.

The appeals court determines whether there is *any evidence supporting* the fact-finding made by the lower court. It applies the utmost deference to the finding made by the judge in reaching its own determination.

There are two separate "no evidence" claims: (1) a matter of law and/or (2) no evidence to support the finding by the trial judge.

When you have suffered an adverse ruling and have the burden of proof, use a matter of law argument. When you do not have the burden of proof and your client suffers an unfavorable finding, postulate there is no evidence to support the finding of the lower court.

A successful challenge of findings based upon a claim of legal sufficiency of the evidence results in a "reversal" of the judgment—a "home run" result for your client.

E. THE CLEARLY ERRONEOUS RULE (SUBSTANTIAL EVIDENCE)

The substantial evidence and the clearly erroneous standards are very similar standards. By definition, substantial evidence is sufficient findings to compel a conclusive finding. The appeals court applying this standard of review examines the evidence in the light most favorable to the judgment.

For example, Mississippi defines it as evidence credible or reasonable. Montana uses a similar standard of where a reasonable mind may find evidence to support a conclusion.

Similarly, in the state of Washington, the trial court's findings of fact are reviewed for a sufficient quantum of evidence to persuade a reasonable person that a finding of fact is true.

North Dakota applies the clearly erroneous rule. It does not reweigh the evidence, reassess the credibility of the witnesses, or substitute the justices' judgment for the judgment of the trial court. A choice between two adequate views of the evidence is not considered clearly erroneous, and is utilized by the appeals court in the state of Delaware.

Similarly, the state of Michigan concludes a finding is clearly erroneous when, although there is evidence to support it, the reviewing court on the entire record is left with the definite and firm conviction a mistake has been made by the trial court. Alaska, Hawaii, Minnesota, South Dakota, West Virginia, and Wyoming all apply this same terminology.

Substantial and competent evidence is another phrase used. Again, just about any evidence, if it is evidence, is of substance and competence.

F. FACTUAL SUFFICIENCY CHALLENGES

Texas, New York, and the U.S. military courts are the only courts recognizing a less deferential "factual sufficiency" standard. This standard permits the appeals court to actually weigh competing and conflicting evidence.

Insufficient evidence or factual insufficiency is when the lower court's finding is against the weight of the evidence and the resulting error is manifestly wrong. When the appeals court determines this error, the appropriate remedy is a reversal.

Practice Pointer

Identify the standard of review early in your review of the matter.

G. ENHANCED BURDENS OF PROOF

All states require a "clear and convincing evidence" to terminate a parent–child relationship. The application of this standard is a good example of an "enhanced burden of proof."

When confronted with an appeal that contains a higher burden of proof, closely analyze your local jurisdiction's higher appellate standard of review. Nationwide, the standards of appellate review for those enhanced burdens of proof are inconsistent.

Here are some examples of enhanced burdens of proof.

In Ohio, a court of appeals in a parental termination case affirms the lower court's findings of fact, if the record contains competent credible evidence by which the trial court can form a belief or conviction that the essential statutory elements are established.

Other states, such as Kansas, Maine, and Wyoming, require a "highly probable" standard in addressing parental termination cases. Other states do not set aside a lower court's judgment unless it is clearly erroneous.

H. ABUSE OF DISCRETION

The abuse of discretion standard of review is universally applied to family law appeals. Most of your appeals are evaluated against this standard, including property division, child custody, alimony, and child support.

Think of this standard as whether the judge acted reasonably in fashioning her decision.

But "reasonableness" with great deference to the trial courts' judgment issued. Ask whether no reasonable judge could reach the same conclusion of the trial judge.

If the answer is no, then you are on to something.

But it is a difficult standard to meet and expose the challenges in family law appellate practice.

Virtually all pretrial rulings and evidentiary rulings are reviewed for an abuse of discretion. Often an abuse of discretion standard is paraphrased as, "Would any reasonable judge have made the same determination?"

I. FAMILY LAW SPECIFIC STANDARDS OF REVIEW

A handful of states employ more than one standard of review in certain family law matters. For example, the state of Maryland employs three standards of review for child custody:

1. When the appellate court reviews factual findings, then the clearly erroneous standard is applied.
2. If it appears the court erred as to matters of law, then the matter is remanded to the trial court. The exception is if the error was harmless.
3. When the appellate court finds that the ultimate conclusion of the lower court is sound and based on factual findings not clearly erroneous, the court's decision is not disturbed unless there is a clear abuse of discretion in the judgment.

J. CLIENT'S UNDERSTANDING OF STANDARDS OF APPELLATE REVIEW

Clients want the appeals court to understand and rehear the facts to show how the judge got it wrong in his or her decision. Inform your client what standard is to be utilized by the reviewing court and how the particular standard may be applied to the facts to your client's case.

Likewise, provide your client an understanding of *what an appeal is and what an appeal is not.* For example, an appeal does not give your client an opportunity to have the reviewing court retry his case. An appeal is not for correcting trial mistakes in presenting evidence.

You want your client to understand appellate courts do not re-decide the case or choose who had the better lawyer. It is your job to educate your client on an understanding of not only the appellant procedure, but also the substantive nature of an appeal and importance of the standards of review.

K. THE REVIEW OF THE FACTS

With very few exceptions, appellate courts presume sufficient facts were presented to the trial judge to support factual decisions the trial judge made. It is only when the appellate court determines the trial judge did not have testimony or evidence sufficient to support a particular "material" finding will the appellate court then consider the trial judge made an error in his or her reliance of the facts at trial. This is an exalting bar for you to reach, as the evidence is viewed most favorable to your opponent.

Usually the reviewing court is concerned with the evidence supporting the trial court's findings and ignores any evidence in support of contrary findings by the trial court.

When you have an opportunity to argue that no evidence exists in the record on appeal, and it is a rare occasion, the appeals court reviews the findings of fact to determine if the judge violated his or her duty to ensure sufficient evidence to support the entered judgment.

L. REVIEWING DISCRETION

Appellate courts apply strong preference to the determinations of the trial judge. It is the trial judge, after all, who was the one who observed and heard the parties during the presentation of the case. He or she was the one in the best position to get what was really going on, so to speak. In fact, the lower court's opinion regarding the credibility and tenor of a witness's credibility is taken as irrefutable.

Abuse of discretion or clearly erroneous or arbitrary and capricious standards of review are all high burdens to meet when you are representing the appellant.

You are attempting to show that the trial judge made the wrong call. This is an exalting standard applied to a judge's discretionary decision.

M. JURISPRUDENTIAL SIGNIFICANCE

Another factor to assess is whether your matter implicates a question of "jurisprudential importance" beyond the immediate dispute of the parties. This is the feeling your case may be as important to your client as it is to other similarly situated litigants.

To assess the jurisprudential significance of your matter, ask:

1. Is there dissent in the court of appeals on your legal issue?
2. Is there a conflict between two or more courts on your legal issue?
3. Does your case involve the construction of a statute? This is particularly true if you are faced with a new statute, such as a new alimony code or update to child support factors.
4. Does your case trigger a state constitutional question?
5. Has the court of appeals made an error of law in a prior decision your matter could now correct?
6. Has the court of appeals decided your issue, but it has not been weighed upon by highest court of your state?

When there are conflicts among lower courts on your legal question, your case can be meaningful.

In addition, if your case raises an interesting question of family law, then its compelling circumstances can cause your state's highest court to grant you review.

N. ERROR CORRECTION

A striking and demonstrative error made by the trial court is the most effective error for obtaining review. Think of this as the cry for "HELP" standard. Argue to the appeals court, emphasizing the potential harm in the error committed by the trial judge. For example, the trial court's error may place a child in danger or violate your client's constitutionally protected rights.

O. SIMILAR CASES

When you are faced with an issue the same as one in another pending case, then point it out. If the court granted review on the merits of the other case with the same issue, explain the similarity to your issue and address it with the court.

You may wish to consult a clerk of the courts to explain the dilemma and seek locally allowed options, such as filing a motion to link the cases.

Some higher courts issue companion opinions disposing of both pending cases. The high court may dispose of the linked petition by way of per curiam, or controlling opinion or its equivalent, depending on the practice in the jurisdiction.

One final standard to consider is that appellate judges sometimes go with his or her own *gut reaction.* Judges bring life experience to your case. They understand the legal issues and likely encountered the same issues before, even if they do not know the facts of your particular case.

Once they have the opportunity to read your well-written brief, they are likely to form an impression and a feeling based upon the life experience they bring to the matter.

If the judges are left with the gnawing sense your client got a raw deal, it is much easier to reverse the case on appeal. Likewise, if the result seems fair or reasonable in light of the facts, it is far easier to obtain an affirmance.

PRACTICE POINTER

Follow your gut when you consider taking on an appeal for a potential client.

Consider the same in your review: *What does your gut tell you about the possibility of an appeal?*

P. CONCLUSION

In summary, understand the applicable standard of review from the beginning of your consideration of a potential appeal. Be familiar with all types of "standards of review" applicable to your case and identify the standard likely to be employed by the appeals court. Once identified, it focuses you on what is truly important in your argument and your argument in turn starts on the right track.

6 Effective Use of Post-Trial Remedies

There are a number of post-trial remedies to correct an error in the trial court's judgment, which can negate your decision to appeal for your client. These are post-trial motions and the availability of stays of the judgment pending appeal that should be considered and filed in certain circumstances. Post-trial remedies are discussed in this chapter.

If you prevail on a post-trial motion, there is no need to pursue an appeal. A post-trial motion can result in a more favorable ruling than the initial order and/or judgment. Or, a note of caution, you may give the judge a chance to clean up a decision.

There are specific rules regarding timing and service of post-trial motions. Check your state and local rules, as many of these motions require shorter time limits for filings, such as only 10 or 14 days from the date the judgment is docketed.

But universally, the filing of post-trial motions affects the validity of your notice of appeal: whereby these *motions may invalidate the notice requiring an additional notice after the resolution of these motions by the trial court.*

Let's first examine applicable post-trial motion to correct a trial court's judgment.

A. A MOTION TO ALTER OR AMEND A JUDGMENT

A motion to amend or alter the judgment may be a better option for your client than an appeal when the judge's order is unclear, confusing, or ambiguous. (This was once called a *motion to reconsider* in some jurisdictions that mirror the federal rules of civil procedure.) You seek relief from the judge to clarify the order without needing to file an appeal.

For example, your client Billy owns two properties in the same condominium complex with his wife, Jean, in Cape Cod: Unit 20 and Unit 31.

After trial, the judge orders Billy to "convey all his interest in the condominium down in Cape Cod to Jean, his now former spouse."

Jean views the judgment as granting to her both condominiums. Billy believes the judge likely made an error by failing to recognize and divide both condominium units by simply giving one to each party.

Rather than file an appeal for Billy, file a motion to amend judgment to find out what the judge intended by pointing out the obvious: there are two condominiums to divide, and each party should receive only one.

The trial judge should recognize the problem and grant the motion. The advantage here is obvious: without appealing a property division, you can solve the issue at hand.

B. MOTION TO AMEND FINDINGS OF FACTS AND CONCLUSIONS OF LAW

Most jurisdictions permit filing a motion to amend findings of fact and/or judgment, or conclusions of law. These motions ask the lower court for a fresh review at the evidence and to "think again" about its decision.

This is often a difficult ask of a trial judge—to persuade him or her to take another look at a case already considered and adjudicated.

With clogged court dockets and too many cases too handle, family law judges do not want to revisit cases on which they have previously ruled. But in the event there is a compelling finding a judge may have missed, it may be worth a chance.

For example, take a child support case, where the judge failed to make a finding, despite evidence, of a party's income. A motion can correct the mistake without the necessity of a potentially costly appeal.

Likewise, jurisdictions permit the filing of motion for More Specific Findings. This type of motion is designed to "beef" up the judgment. Keep in mind appellate courts will presume the lower court made coordinated findings in support of the judgment. By asking for more specific findings, and when they do not still hold water on appeal, then you can seek an appellate ruling that the findings were insufficient. On the other hand, a more sufficient judgment may result in the greater likelihood of an affirmance. Consider both results before filing.

C. MOTION FOR A NEW TRIAL

A court grants a new trial "by reason of some accident, mistake, or misfortune in the conduct of the trial so a new trial is necessary to prevent a failure of justice."[24]

Reasons to grant a new trial include findings contrary to the weight of evidence, newly discovered evidence, legal error by the trial judge, misconduct affecting the judgment, and the death or disability of the trial judge.

If the court allows the motion for a new trial, it may do the following:

1. Open the judgment.
2. Take additional testimony.

---

24. Charles P. Kindregan, Monroe L. Inker & Patricia A. Kindregan, Family Law and Practice (2A *Massachusetts Practice Series*) § 56:8 (4th ed.) (citing *Davis v. Boston Elevated Ry. Co.*, 235 Mass. 482, 486, 1920).

3. Amend findings of fact and conclusions of law.
4. Make new findings of fact and conclusions of law.

Or

5. Direct the entry of a new judgment.

All of the above saves time and costs for your client and can result in the avoidance of filing and prosecuting an appeal.

D. CLERICAL ERRORS

What if the judgment appears different from what the judge told your client and related parties in open court?

For example, the wife receives the marital home in the final written judgment, where the parties agreed the husband would retain it and the judge agreed to enter this agreement in open court.

Jurisdictions allow for the correction of inadvertent errors or mistakes in the judgment. These may be corrected by the court itself sua sponte or upon filing a motion with the trial judge.

If you are seeking to correct a judge's minor error in the judgment, consider filing a motion to correct the clerical error. This is surely a faster avenue than filing an appeal.

PRACTICE POINTER

After receipt of the lower court's judgment, meet with your client to discuss postjudgment motions prior to filing a notice of appeal.

E. OTHER POST-TRIAL REMEDIES

A court can provide postjudgment relief for a party from a final judgment, order, or proceeding for the following reasons:

1. Mistake, inadvertence, surprise, or excusable neglect.
2. Newly discovered evidence, which by due diligence could not have been discovered in time to move for a motion for a new trial under.

3. Fraud (whether heretofore denominated intrinsic or extrinsic), misrepresentation, or other misconduct of an adverse party.
4. The judgment is void.
5. The judgment is satisfied, released, or discharged, or a prior judgment upon which it is based is reversed or otherwise vacated, or it is no longer equitable the judgment should have prospective application; or
6. Any other reason justifying relief from the operation of the judgment.

You should note this "catchall" provision does not circumvent the times limits of 1 through 3. All of these motions require specific time guidelines for filing.

The court is afforded broad discretion in determining whether to grant these post-trial motions. Moreover, a judge's ruling on motions for fraud, mistake, and newly discovered evidence is reversed on appeal only by showing an abuse of discretion.

Federal Rule of Civil Procedure 60, which is mimicked in most local rules, is a useful tool to set aside judgments when the evidence suggests an opposing party concealed assets or has committed fraud upon the court.

An example is when your adverse party files a false financial affidavit the trial court has relied upon in issuing its judgment. If you are able to easily prove such bad conduct, then it is better practice to seek relief from the judge before you seek appellate relief.

Practice Pointer

If there has been fraudulent conduct by an adverse party, an alternative remedy to a rule 60 motion might be an equity action to divide an undisclosed asset.

Similarly, a Rule 60 motion regarding fraud can be brought in connection with whether the opposing party knew the actual value of an asset at the time of the divorce and failed to properly disclose it.

Now let's examine the effect a properly filed post-trial motion can have upon the timing and validity of the notice of appeal.

F. THE EFFECT OF POST-TRIAL MOTIONS ON THE NOTICE OF APPEAL

Be familiar with your local rules on the effect a filing of a post-trial motion has on the notice of appeal.

In many jurisdictions, when a party timely files a post-trial motion under the local equivalent of Federal Rules 52(b) or 59, then the time for appeal for all parties shall run from ***the entry of the order denying a new trial or granting or denying any other such motion. In other words, a Rule 52 or Rule 59 motion makes a final order no longer final.***

Various other post-trial motions do *not* stay the appeal period: Federal Rule 60 motions (or the local Rule 60), motions for clarification, and motions for reconsideration, if allowed by jurisdiction, generally do not stay the time to file a notice of appeal.

Follow your local rules regarding the timing of your notice of appeal.

But the critical point: *A notice of appeal filed before the disposition of any of the above motions* (Federal Rule 60 motions or the local Rule 60, motions for clarification, and motions for reconsideration) *shall have no effect.* Therefore, ***a new notice of appeal must be filed within the prescribed time measured from the entry of the order disposing of the motion.*** A premature notice of appeal is as if no notice of appeal was filed at all.

In many jurisdictions, where a judgment enters before the trial court issues findings, you must file a notice of appeal within thirty days after the judgment enters. You may not rely on a Federal Rule 52(b) motion regarding findings issued postjudgment to stay the appeal period.

This means when you receive the judgment and the judge promised to provide the parties "findings" at a later date, you must file your notice of appeal within thirty days of receiving the judgment and not thirty days after receipt of the findings.

PRACTICE POINTER

If you have any doubt as to whether the appeal period has been properly extended as a result of the filing of a motion under rule 52(b) or 59, file a notice of appeal within the required time period regardless. If it is premature, it is void and no harm is done. If the motions did not for some reason stay the appeals period, then you timely filed your notice.

G. EXPEDITE APPEALS FOR CHILDREN

States may allow by right expedited appeals in matters involving children.

Expedite an appeal if you are representing the party who loses a custody decision, such as a removal action of a child out of state.

If you are seeking to expedite an appeal, obtain a determination on a properly filed post-trial motion as soon as possible from the trial judge.

Always check with your local court if you are unsure of local rules regarding the determination of post-trial motions and the scheduling procedure of the court.

In general, courts and judges do not automatically schedule a hearing on postjudgment motions.

The granting of a hearing on these motions can be discretionary by the trial judge. If necessary, you may need to be a "thorn in the side" of the clerk to ensure your post-trial motion is scheduled and decided by the trial judge.

PRACTICE POINTER

If you are likely to appeal an issue and your judge is likely to deny any post-trial relief, an appeal may be the only option.

H. SUSPENSION OF THE JUDGMENT

In most situations, the appeal of a judgment does stay the enforcement of a judgment.

Take poor Ralph.

He is hit with an alimony judgment well over and above his present ability to pay to his ex-spouse. Well, Ralph may still have to pay the alimony ordered during the pendency of the appeal.

The majority of jurisdictions have adopted statues where an appeal does not stay the operation of any aspects of the divorce judgment relative to custody, visitation, alimony, support, or maintenance.

So, what do you do for Ralph?

File a motion to stay the judgment pending the appeal.

A motion to stay is filed in the lower court that issued the judgment. If denied by the lower court, a motion to stay the judgment pending appeal is then filed in the appeals court. Use the drafting of the motion as an additional opportunity to begin to frame your case.

Take the following example.

The lower court ordered the sale of the husband's family home of over one hundred fifty years, despite the parties' brief marriage of only three years. The husband has sufficient assets to buy out the wife, but the lower court abused its discretion in ordering its sale.

In addition, the husband offered to bond the home's value pending appeal. Thus, file a motion asking to stay the order of the sale of the marital home pending the husband's appeal.

A request to stay the judgment sets forth any reasons in support of the relief sought and includes a discussion of the pertinent facts. Support the motion by affidavits signed under the pains of perjury. Cite the relevant portions of the record.

Relief to stay a judgment may be conditioned upon posting bond or other approved security, in the lower court. Thus in the example above, it is a good idea to request alternative relief from the appeals court to persuade them to grant a stay. The following would work in the example above:

> The husband respectfully requests this Honorable Court *stay the sale of the marital home or at a minimum allow him to post a bond in the market value of the marital as determined by the lower court.*

I. ENFORCEMENT

Trial courts retain jurisdiction for the purpose of enforcement of a judgment and attorney fee awards in some jurisdictions.

Steps to suspend enforcement vary from state to state. Understand the effect of your appeal upon the judgment.

PRACTICE POINTER

If you are seeking a stay of a judgment and it involves property division, request relief by proposing a sufficient bond pending the appeal.

Generally, courts allow a bond to be posted in accordance with applicable state statutes to suspend enforcements of the judgment while you seek your client's appeal. Some jurisdictions allow discretion to the lower court to determine appropriate conditions to protect the interests of the appellee pending an appeal of the judgment.

A bond may not suspend the trial court's order in all respects, including the judgment of divorce. These are often called *supersedeas bonds* and may involve estimates of costs, fees, and judgment.

In some jurisdictions, filing a bond prevents the trial court's enforcement of an order changing child custody. In such jurisdictions, custody issues are subject to the exclusive jurisdiction of the appellate court while the appeal is pending. In these situations, many appellate courts are reluctant to disturb the lower court orders pending an appeal.

It should be noted in those jurisdictions where the trial court lacks the power to enforce a property division pending appeal, this does not permit the appealing party to disregard the court's order.

Inform your client that the judgment must be followed pending appeal. Otherwise, your client could be liable for contempt charges, including costs and fees, and for violations during the pendency of the appeal.

PRACTICE POINTER

Always file a motion to stay concurrently with all other post-trial motions. Perhaps the judge denies your motions but grants, in whole or in part, the request for a stay.

J. THE IMPORTANCE OF A COMPLETE DECISION OR FINAL ORDER

Post-trial proceedings are the time to "clean up" the record by making sure the trial court's decision is clear and all issues requiring adjudication are addressed. This is critical for not only any pending appeal, but also for potential future modification actions. For example, if certain findings are required to be made by the trial court—such as each spouse's income—your appeal is hindered if those findings are missing from the record.

Your appeal can be dismissed or remanded back to the trial court and it all begins again, which would be painful and costly for your client. Not to mention a malpractice claim in the wings.

Further, ensure all motions are ruled on by the trial judge and all written memorandum of decision are obtained to complete the record.

State rules to specify what kind of judgments or orders must be reduced to writing or the extent to which a trial court must explain a decision in writing. For example, findings of fact may or may not be required by local rule. Also, if the decision was issued "verbally" from the bench, then arrangements must be made to obtain the transcript of the decision.

The lower court's findings are critical for preserving your client's rights in future modification actions.

In all states, parties may move for modification of at least some issues based on a material change in circumstance. For example, judgments related to child custody, child support, and alimony are usually modifiable in the future.

States require specific findings at the time of the initial judgment to engage in appellate review of a modification action.

Assume, for example, a wife brings a motion to modify alimony three years after her divorce because her ex-husband now earns substantially more income, but the trial court denies the modification. The basis of the denial is because the original dissolution judgment did not specify the husband's earning income at the time of divorce.

The problem you then encounter is your client, the wife, is not be able to prove a change in circumstance to demonstrate the former husband's income has now increased without the baseline included from the prior judgment.

The failure to shore up your record following the trial can impact not only your appeal, but also any future changes in the initial judgment issued by the lower court.

PRACTICE POINTER

Even when there is no appeal of a judgment, ensure all required findings are entered to preserve a future modification action.

K. THE USE OF POST-TRIAL MOTIONS TO COMPLETE THE RECORD

Post-trial motions are your last opportunity to raise any matters prior to the appeal. The use of a post-trial motion is a potential tool to correct lapses in the record in the trial court. It does not replace a thoroughly created trial record but can add critical issues to the record and help to begin to frame major appellate issues. It may be too late, but it does not hurt to make an attempt.

For many appellate courts, the decisive factor is whether the trial court was provided a fair notice of an issue and an opportunity to decide it correctly. A post-judgment motion might be challenged for timeliness, but you are essentially giving the trial court this one last chance to "get it right."

But keep in mind such a step can be a double-edged sword.

Although it may provide the trial judge with an opportunity to clarify your record for a potential appeal, it may provide the trial judge with an opportunity to shore up the original decision to make it more "appeal proof." Or even worse, the trial judge may alter the judgment against your client.

Let's review other possible stays affecting your client's appeal.

L. OTHER POSSIBLE STAYS

Family law is state specific. This local nature is particularly true when it comes to the availability of stays of judgments in family law. But there are some judgment stays applicable in all local rules. These include bankruptcy proceedings, stays pursuant to the Uniform Child Custody Jurisdiction and Enforcement Act (UCCJEA) and stays available to members of the U.S. military.

M. BANKRUPTCY

When your client or the opposing party in your case files a petition for bankruptcy, an automatic stay takes effect and establishes a level of protection preventing any and all actions held by creditors from acquiring the debtor's assets. The filing of a bankruptcy action by a litigant in your case presents implications and exceptions in relation to the nondebtor spouse's rights. It is important to be familiar with the effects of a bankruptcy filing whether you represent the debtor or the nondebtor litigant.

The Bankruptcy Code provides an exception from the automatic stay in the context of a divorce proceeding, which allows an individual to commence or continue a suit for divorce.[25] Although a party may file for divorce or pursue a divorce filing, bankruptcy stays prevent the distribution of any property that falls within the bankruptcy estate.[26]

Within this exception, you must review local state laws to determine the ability to proceed to a final judgment of divorce.

The family law exceptions to the automatic stay in bankruptcy can include not only the court's ability to dissolve the marriage, but also implementation of a child custody order, parenting time, child support, and alimony.

---

25. 11 U.S.C.A § 362(b)(2)(A)(iv).

26. *Id.*

Be familiar with the effect on the property division in the final judgment when you are seeking to appeal the judgment of the lower court.

When a notice of bankruptcy is filed with the applicable court of appeals, the bankruptcy action automatically stays the appeal. This prevents the distribution of what would otherwise be the now separate property of the nondebtor spouse.

However, the nondebtor spouse may seek relief by filing a motion to lift the stay in the bankruptcy court, which would then allow the appeal to continue.

Likewise, if you are representing the nondebtor spouse and your motion is successful, you can execute the judgment to enforce the property division by the lower court.

You can then claim your client's portion of the marital estate free and clear of the remaining creditors in the bankruptcy filing.

N. UCCJEA

The UCCJEA has been adopted by all states, except Massachusetts, which has adopted the prior version (UCCJA).[27] There are two provisions in the UCCJEA providing mechanisms to stay otherwise valid proceedings.

The first is where there are "simultaneous proceedings" in more than one state. The second is when one state is an "inconvenient forum" to hear the action.

When there are two simultaneous proceedings in two states, the determination of which forum has "home state jurisdiction" takes top priority in evaluating the proper court to proceed.

If the trial court determines it does not have home state jurisdiction, it is then obligated to stay its own proceedings and communicate with the other state to determine which state is the appropriate venue to address the matter.

In this scenario, it is important for you to assess your individual state statutes regarding home state jurisdiction. Your state's

27. Both versions adopt similar rules for the determination of "home state jurisdiction" of a child but Massachusetts has not adopted the concept of "continuing jurisdiction" over the matter.

version of the UCCJEA addresses the scenario when neither state's requirements for home state jurisdiction are met.

In addition, a judge may determine his or her state is an inconvenient forum, even though it is the court with home state jurisdiction. The judge may also determine there is actually no home state for the children.

In determining whether the state is an inconvenient forum, a trial judge considers the usual factors of significant contacts with the forum, the location of evidence, the location of witnesses, and other pertinent factors contained with your specific state statutes to assess the appropriate forum.

If and when the judge determines a state is an inconvenient forum, he or she can stay the court's proceedings to allow the parties to file an action in the more appropriate state. If such an action is not filed, or if the other state declines to accept jurisdiction, the first state will dissolve its stay and continue the proceeding.

If you are on the wrong end of such a decision, a review of the trial court's decision may be available by an immediate writ to a superior court or an appeal to your higher court, depending on your state laws governing such decisions.

Be aware of the appropriate procedure to seek appellate relief when it is warranted and to act timely due to the potential loss of jurisdiction over the matter for your client.

O. MILITARY

Servicemembers Civil Relief Act of 2003 (SCRA) was enacted to protect the legal rights of individuals serving in the armed forces of the United States.

The stated purpose of the Act is to "suspend enforcement of civil liabilities in certain cases of persons in the military service of the United States to enable such persons to devote their entire energy to the defense needs of the nation."[28]

Under the SCRA, if you have a client who is engaged in active military service, you may request a stay at any stage during a civil

28. 50 App. U.S.C.A. §§ 501–596.

action. The request of a stay includes an appeal of a divorce or child custody proceeding.

The court has the authority to grant a stay on its own motion, sua sponte, and must grant the motion upon timely application filed by your client, if it finds the service member's ability to participate in the suit is materially affected by his or her active military service.

The court may impose limitations and conditions upon the stay if issued by the court. For example, the court can order your client to make arrangements for leave or travel to participate in the pending proceedings.

P. WEIGHING ALL OPTIONS

In summary, prior to the filing of any appeal, review with your client all applicable post-trial remedies; then consider the temperament of your judge and the likelihood of correcting the judgment short of filing an appeal with a reviewing court. Always be realistic with your client, and if there is a reasonable chance of success of a well-crafted post-trial motion, then it should be pursued.

Keep in mind even if the relief sought is denied, you are not waiving your client's right to later appeal, just prolonging the timing of the appeal until the judge rules on the post-trial motion(s).

Be mindful that the mere act of appealing does not necessarily stay the operation of the judgment. A post-trial motion to alter or amend a judgment or for a new trial will affect the validity of the notice of appeal. This will require a new notice of appeal only after the trial court's disposition of these motions.

Finally, along with your assessment of all post-trial remedies, review your options concerning any available stays affecting the appeal and/or assist your client during the pendency of his or her appeal.

7 The Notice of Appeal: Form, Contents, and Time

Every appeal begins with a NOTICE OF APPEAL. You must properly format and timely file it or run the risk of your appeal becoming null and void. The battle is lost, the client is unhappy, and you have an issue with your malpractice carrier.

You need to be familiar with how to file and serve the appropriate notice of appeal. Thereafter, you have to ensure the appeal itself is "perfected" and placed on the docket in the appellate court.

The purpose of a notice of appeal is to provide your opponent fair notice that you are seeking review of the lower court's order or judgment to a higher court.

The "jurisdictional significance" of the notice of appeal divests the trial court of jurisdiction as to those issues raised in your client's appeal. This jurisdictional transfer from the lower court to the higher court of appeals assumes the appeal has been taken from an appealable judgment of a final order.

If you file a notice of appeal from a nonappealable order or if you fail to properly perfect the notice of appeal, the transfer of the matter to the appeals court can be a nullity.

All courts implement rules specifying the content of what belongs within a notice of appeal. Despite the seemingly straightforward nature of these rules, there is no shortage of notices of appeal not complying with the applicable rules, leading to the dismissal of the appeal. As a result, a word of caution: Be very familiar with your local rules and draft with care your notice of appeal in each matter.

A reminder: there is no substitute for knowing your local rules of how and when to file the notice of appeal.

A. THE TECHNICAL REQUIREMENTS

1. Where?

Know *where* the notice of appeal is filed in your client's case. The proper place for filing is usually the trial court, but some jurisdictions require a notice of appeal to be filed within the appeals court.

For example, the state of Colorado requires a notice of appeal be filed with the appellate court with a copy served upon the clerk of the trial court. Likewise, in New Jersey, an appeal is initiated by filing the original notice within the appellate division and a copy goes to the trial court. In Oklahoma, the original notice of appeal is filed within the appeals court.

Regardless of the rule, it is critical to ensure you file in the correct court, since the commencement of an appeal is a jurisdictional event, and failing to file in the right place can result in waiving your client's appellate rights.

Practice Pointer

If there is any confusion as to where to file the notice of appeal, confirm with a clerk of the appellate court.

What happens when you file the notice of an appeal within the wrong court?

This is something, of course, you would never do; however, you may have a pro se litigant come to you for an appeal, after the notice itself has been filed, and you learn it was filed in the wrong court.

Do not panic.

If a notice of appeal is mistakenly filed in the court of appeals, most state rules allow the clerk to indicate on the notice the date when it was received and send it to the proper trial court for entry on the docket. The notice of appeal is then considered filed in its proper place.

PRACTICE POINTER

To be safe, file a motion to be permitted to file the appeal even if the motion is untimely under your local rules.

B. CONTENTS

The notice of appeal itself is not a difficult filing. The content of a notice of appeal is prescribed by court rules or statute.

In the federal system, for example, a notice of appeal contains three required elements: (1) the party appealing, (2) what is being appealed, and (3) the name of the court you are seeking for your appeal.[29]

States have differing requirements. California requires only a notice of appeal that identifies the judgment or order being appealed. You are not required to notice the specific court to which the appeal is being taken.[30] Instead, the California rule presumes an appeal is being taken to the appropriate appellate district in which the superior court is located.

29. Federal Rule of Appellate Procedure Rule 3.
30. California Rules of Court, Rule 8.100(a) (2).

Oklahoma entitles a notice of appeal a "Petition in Error." It provides a form for its rather lengthy list of required information for a notice of appeal.[31]

Massachusetts requires that a notice of appeal be a written statement prepared and filed in the trial court. You are required to include (1) the name of your case, (2) the trial court docket number, (3) and your intention to appeal the judgment.[32]

Some states require notice of the judgment, specifically, you are taking appeal from. So, if you want to take appeal of the initial judgment and those judgments post-trial, some require broad language to include all of them.

The notice of appeal includes your name and contact information and specifies the order, decree, or judgment that you are appealing.

In general, and fortunately, when determining whether an appellant has complied with the requirements for a notice of appeal, courts employ a rule of "liberal construction." Courts prefer to hear an appeal on its merits, unless there is a substantive jurisdictional defect.

C. THE NOTICE ITSELF

First, every notice of appeal identifies the party or parties taking the appeal. But what happens if the notice of appeal does not do so?

In *Torres v. Oakland Scavenger Company*, 487 U.S. 312 (1988), the U.S. Supreme Court ruled a notice of appeal naming fifteen plaintiffs, but not a sixteenth, did not confer jurisdiction on the court of appeals over the unnamed plaintiff, despite the notice of appeal's use of the term *et al.*

Noting that the purpose of a notice of appeal is to reveal the appellants' identities to the opposing party and to the court, the court said "the use of the phrase 'et al.,' which literally means

31. Oklahoma Supreme Court Rules 1.23(a)(1), 1.25, 1.301 (form 5).
32. Massachusetts Rules of Appellate Procedure Rule 3.

'and others' utterly fails to provide such notice to either intended recipient."[33]

The Supreme Court rejected what is referred to as the normal rule of liberal construction of notices of appeal, on the theory that by doing so would enlarge the jurisdictional time period for filing a notice of appeal by a party who was not named in the original notice.[34]

After the Supreme Court decided *Torres*, Rule 3 of the Federal Rules of Appellate Procedure was amended due to the harsh results arising from the Supreme Court's interpretation of Rule 3(c) in *Torres*.

Today, the Federal Rule provides the requirement of specifying who is appealing may be accomplished by "naming each one in the caption or body of the notice, but an attorney representing more than one party may describe those parties with such terms as 'all plaintiffs,' 'the defendants,' 'the plaintiffs A, B, et al.,' or 'all defendants except X.'"[35]

The advisory committee said that "the test established by the rule for determining whether such designations are sufficient is whether it is objectively clear that a party intended to appeal."[36]

D. PRO SE AND NOTICES

Many family law appeals are started or taken by a pro se litigant who is unfamiliar with the intricacies of appellate practice. If you are defending such an appeal, you may wish to attack the notice itself, but keep in mind most states follow the liberal approach to the notice filing.

For example, a notice of appeal filed by a pro se party is deemed filed on behalf of the party signing the notice unless the notice clearly indicates a contrary intent.

---

33. Torres v. Oakland Scavenger Company, 487 U.S. 312 at 318.

34. *Id.*

35. Federal Rules Appellate Procedure Rule 3, *Advisory Committee Notes* (1993).

36. *Id.*

E. TYPICAL NOTICE MISTAKES

Lawyers—not you, but other lawyers—make errors in the drafting of a notice of appeal. The policy favoring liberal construction of a notice of appeal will only get you so far if you make an unlikely error.

The Second Circuit has held naming the appealing party in the caption only is not necessarily sufficient to confer jurisdiction within the appeals court.[37]

The court reasoned a notice of appeal fails to comply with Rule 3's requirement to specify the party or parties taking the appeal where the body of the notice states someone else is taking the appeal. A harsh result, but instructive for you of the importance of carefully drafting the notice of appeal.

F. NOTICE CONTENTS

The notice of appeal identifies each appealable judgment or order your client is seeking to appeal. This is critical for you, the family law attorney.

Let's take an example.

Your client is unhappy with a divorce judgment from the trial court. But the same client is very pleased with the divorce—finally—and thrilled she also received the house from the marital division judgment of the trial judge. But this very same client is also quite angry about the miniscule amount of alimony awarded by the very same trial judge.

What to do?

Craft the appeal to address only what *you are seeking to change in the appeal court.* If you are only challenging the alimony award, then that is the only order that you are appealing. You do not need to challenge the property division.

The only caveat here is if the alimony award interplays with the division of marital assets. In that event, you would indeed challenge both parts of the judgment.

37. Gusler v. City of Long Beach, 700 F.3d 646, 648 (2d Cir. 2012).

Appellate courts do not want to alter lower court judgments in family law matters in particular. So you limit what you challenge *to only what should be challenged.*

Use the notice of appeal to make clear to the appeals court that you are only seeking what really needs to be changed in light of both the facts and the law. Be specific and direct with your drafting of the notice of appeal.

PRACTICE POINTER

A family law notice of appeal should be limited to only the matter you are seeking an appeal of and no ancillary matters.

G. NOTICE OF APPEAL EXAMPLE

THE STATE

THE TRIAL COURT

PROBATE AND FAMILY COURT DEPARTMENT

NAME OF DIVISION	**DOCKET NO. THE DOCKET**
THE WIFE'S NAME Plaintiff v. THE HUSBAND'S NAME Defendant	

THE PLAINTIFF'S NOTICE OF APPEAL OF SUPPLEMENTAL JUDGMENT OF DIVORCE NISI DATED (ALWAYS FILL IN) AND DOCKETED (ALWAYS FILL IN) BY (NAME OF COURT) PROBATE COURT (NAME OF JUDGE) ON A COMPLAINT FOR DIVORCE (DATE OF FILING)

NOTICE IS HEREBY GIVEN THAT PLAINTIFF (**party name**), in the above-captioned matter, hereby appeals to the Appeals Court the Supplemental Judgment of Divorce Nisi dated (**fill in**) and docked (**fill in**) by the (**name of court**) Probate and Family Court **(name of judge**) J. on a Complaint for Divorce (**filing date**).

Plaintiff appeals the decision of (**name of judge**) of the supplemental judgment dated (**date**) in provision numbers 1–4 as follows:

1. Commencing on November 28, 2014, and each Friday thereafter, the Husband shall pay alimony to Wife in the amount of $500. The Husband's alimony obligation to the Wife shall terminate upon the death of either party; the Wife's remarriage; or 95 months from November 28, 2014, whichever shall occur first.

2. For as long as Husband continues to have any obligation to pay the Wife alimony he shall maintain and regularly pay the premiums on a life insurance policy on his life with death benefits totaling no less than $250,000, naming Wife as the beneficiary. He shall provide the Wife with proof of said insurance on or before April 1, 2015.
3. The Husband shall pay the Wife all alimony arrears owed to her from November 28, 2014, through the date of this judgment, by April 1, 2015.
4. Each party shall pay his or her own attorney's fees.

Dated: (date of notice) Respectfully submitted.

(Name of party) the Plaintiff
By her Attorney,

____

(Your Name) BBO
(Firm Name)
(Address)
(Address)
(Telephone Number) (Fax Number)
(E-Mail)

CERTIFICATE OF SERVICE

The undersigned hereby certifies that a true copy of the within Plaintiff's/Appellant's Notice of Appeal was this day served upon Defendant by mailing same, first class postage prepaid, to his Counsel, (name) of (firm name) located at (address).

Dated: (Date of Notice)

____

(Your Signature)

Some jurisdictions will accept a broadly worded written notice. For example, "I appeal from the judgment." This type of notice captures a wide net and is sufficient. Likewise, "I appeal the Docket Entry of March 23, 2018, and all orders leading to and arising from that Docket Entry."

H. OTHER NOTICE CONSIDERATIONS AND POTENTIAL TRAPS

State that you are taking an appeal of the final judgment in your properly drafted notice of appeal. This is true even if you plan to challenge an error on appeal committed by an interlocutory ruling. Courts theorize that all interlocutory orders preceding the final judgment "merge" into the final judgment. Therefore, these prejudgment orders may be reviewed on appeal without separately identifying them in the notice of appeal.

This approach makes logical sense because most interlocutory orders are by definition nonappealable, so why would you need to specify nonappealable orders in your notice of appeal?

There are several potential traps for you to consider in your notice drafting.

First, where a case is dismissed for failure to prosecute the action, any issued interlocutory orders do not merge into the final judgment. Therefore, these orders may not be reviewed on appeal from the order of dismissal. For example, when a party receives a temporary child support order under a modification action later dismissed.

Second, some prejudgment orders may be separately appealable. For example, you may have the option of appealing an interlocutory or temporary child custody order. In fact, in some jurisdictions, failure to appeal from such an appealable order when it is made precludes review of that order on a later appeal from the judgment.[38]

Third, where the appeal is not taken from the final judgment but from "a specified judgment or part of a specified judgment," courts are less likely to allow challenges on appeal to orders not specified in the notice of appeal.[39]

---

38. In re Marriage of Lloyd, 55 Cal.App.4th 216, 219 (1997).
39. Markham v. Holt, 369 F.2d 940, 942 (5th Cir. 1966).

Finally, postjudgment orders appealed must be identified in a timely notice of appeal, as they are not reviewable on appeal taken solely from the judgment.

The most common example for you in family law matters is awards of your attorneys' fees issued by the trial judge, but after the judgment is entered.

I. TIME STANDARDS OF FILING THE NOTICE

Know the appropriate time standards in your jurisdiction as to when you must file the notice of appeal. The time standards run the gamut from ten to thirty days.

The rule of timely filing a notice of appeal is "draconian." Think Darth Vader.

Failure to timely file the notice of appeal can result in the dismissal of your client's appeal. It is considered in civil cases a *jurisdictional requirement*. Therefore, if the notice of appeal is not filed in the time set out in your local rules, the court of appeal has no jurisdiction to hear the appeal. As a result, the appeal is dismissed.

PRACTICE POINTER

When you first receive a judgment from the lower court, immediately contact the lower court to find out if the judgment has been docketed so you can determine in your initial conversations with your client how many days you have to file a notice of appeal.

Every family law attorney understands the litigation must eventually come to an end. This is precisely the reasoning behind the importance of court's adhering to strict time mandates in the filing of notice of appeals. It is to set the exact time for when litigation is *over* and to allow the court to expedite appeals free of gamesmanship from any party.

The U.S. Supreme Court put it this way:

> The purpose of the rule is clear: It is "to set a definite point of time when litigation shall be at an end, unless within that time the prescribed application has been made; and if it has not, to

advise prospective appellees that they are freed of the appellant's demands. Any other construction of the statute would defeat its purpose."[40]

J. THE USUAL TIME

In federal courts, the normal time to file a notice of appeal is thirty (30) days after the entry of judgment upon the docket.[41] Most states adopt similar timing. The timing to file the notice of appeal is important, but equally critical is to understand *how the entry of judgment* is defined by your local rules.

Appellate procedure defines *entry* in different ways, depending upon which rules have been adopted by your local jurisdiction.

But the key term for you to understand and adhere to is *entry,* not *notice of entry*.

In other words, the time to file your notice of appeal begins not from the time you received the notice of the judgment, but from entry of the judgment within the court. Thus it is incumbent on you to determine in every instance when a judgment is actually entered by the court, a topic discussed next.

Consider the following.

You receive the judgment and the judge herself dated it: August 28, 2017.

You think, *Okay, well, I have time from August 28, 2017, forward to file my client's notice of appeal.* Well, the answer is not yes or no but actually "maybe."

If your jurisdiction rule is a notice of an appeal must be filed within thirty days of entry of judgment, the date written by the trial judge on the judgment has zero meaning. Contact the trial court to inquire as to when the docket entry was *actually made, not the date of the judgment itself* as written by the trial judge.

If the court has not yet entered the judgment onto the docket, then your thirty-day clock has not commenced. If the court has in

40. Coleman v. Thompson, 501 U.S. 722, 751 (1991).

41. Federal Rule of Appellate Procedure Rule 4.

fact entered the case on the docket, say September 7, then you have thirty days thereafter.

PRACTICE POINTER

When a judgment has not been entered into the docket, consult the clerk to determine when the judgment may enter but also request the judgment is entered on the docket so you can file your notice of appeal.

Once again, every jurisdiction has its own rules and you must consult the rules for the jurisdiction in which the appeal is taken.

For example, California has alternative periods, depending on whether a party or the clerk of the court has given written notice of entry of the appealable judgment or order.

In that event, the time to appeal is shorter (60 days from service of notice of entry) than the time if no formal notice has been served (180 days if no service of formal notice of entry).[42]

In New York, an appellant must file a notice of appeal "within thirty days after service by a party upon the appellant of a copy of the judgment or order appealed from and written notice of its entry."[43]

Remain vigilant with your local clerk's office to comply with the applicable rules.

K. NO NOTICE OF APPEAL?

Finally, sometimes even the failure to file a proper notice of appeal is excused. This is often the situation with the notice of appeal filed by a pro se litigant.

Courts have allowed documents, indisputably not notices of appeal, to function as notice of appeal so long as they are timely filed under the rules and provide the minimum information required of a formal notice of appeal.

42. California Rules of Court, Rule 8.104(a) (2017).

43. New York Consolidated Laws, Civil Practice Law and Rules—CVP § 5513.

L. SERVICE OF THE NOTICE OF APPEAL

Once you complete the proper notice and file it with the correct court, understand your next service obligation. The general rule is a party's failure to serve the notice of appeal on the opposing party does not affect its validity.

Under the federal rules and some states, the failure of service of the notice is forgiven. Some jurisdictions require service of the notice of appeal by the clerk of the court rather than the party seeking the appeal of the judgment.

Nevertheless, even if just for the sake of courtesy to opposing counsel, the better practice is to serve the notice of appeal and accompany the filed original with a proof of service.

PRACTICE POINTER

Serve the notice of appeal and file a proof of service even if no rule requires it.

M. THE EVENTS THAT MAY EXTEND TIME

Now for the more difficult part of the filing—the potential effect of post-trial motions on the notice of appeal.

Let's review. You filed your notice of appeal. But you filed a post-trial motion contemporaneously with a notice of appeal.

Here is where you really need to be on your game to avoid dismissal of your appeal and a very angry client who is already likely feeling "screwed by the system."

Some, but not all, post-trial motions extend the time to appeal and invalidate the notice initially filed.

Thus, and this is the difficult part, *a premature notice of appeal may be invalid*. You must therefore understand not only the time constraints for notice of appeals, but also the effect of post-trial motions on the notice of appeal.

The federal system is instructive as states have adopted similar rules. Under federal rules, the time to file your notice of appeal does not start to run where a party files any of the following specific motions:

1. A motion for judgment under Federal Rule 50(b)
2. A motion to amend or to make additional factual findings under Federal Rule 52(b)
3. A motion to alter or amend the judgment under Federal Rule 59
4. A motion for new trial under Federal Rule 59
5. A motion for relief under Federal Rule 60, but only if the motion is made within twenty-eight days after the judgment is entered[44]

Always check your state and local rules when you and/or your opponent file any of the above motions to determine the effect upon the notice of appeal.

In addition, if you bring forth a motion for attorney fees under Federal Rule 54(d) (2) (or your state's equivalent) before a notice of appeal is filed, the trial court may issue an order, which may toll the time to appeal. However, this is not an automatic tolling of time for the notice of appeal, as is the case with the other motions specified above.

Also, be cognizant that a post-trial motion not timely filed does not extend the time to file the notice of appeal; instead the time will run from entry of judgment on the trial court docket.

One trap for you to avoid is to not withdraw your post-trial motion without it being decided, unless you are able to file a notice of appeal within the "normal" time.

Why?

A withdrawn post-trial motion may be treated as a nullity and does not toll the time to appeal a judgment.[45]

N. MOTIONS THAT DO NOT EXTEND THE TIME

Post-trial motions that do not extend the time to file a notice of appeal from the judgment include motions to assess costs and for attorneys' fees.

---

44. Federal Rules of Appellate Procedure Rule 4(a)(4).

45. Vanderwerf v. SmithKline Beecham Corp., 603 F.3d 842 (10th Cir. 2010; Appellate Practice in Federal and State Courts § 5.01 Notice.

A motion for attorneys' fees and costs is not a substantive part of the judgment. It is independent from the cause of the action. Therefore, fees-based motions do not toll the time to seek the appeal of the judgment.

Keep this distinction in mind, as family law trials often result in an award of fees only entered after the entry of the judgment.

O. AMENDED JUDGMENTS

In some cases, even if not prompted by the parties, the trial judge enters an amended judgment. The question to ask is, Does the entry of an amended judgment restart the clock for filing a notice of appeal? The answer is "sometimes."

A nonsubstantive revision of a previously entered judgment does not restart or otherwise affect the period to file your notice of appeal. For example, the correction of a property address of a property division contained in a judgment.

Instead, it is only when your trial judge materially alters the judgment that the time period to file your notice of appeal commences again. For example, the judge, upon further reflection, decides to award the marital home to the husband rather than the wife as originally divided in the marital property division.

P. THE PREMATURE NOTICE

The premature filing of a notice of appeal may happen to you. This is what may happen and this is how to react.

You may file a notice of appeal too early and not too late.

You may file a notice of appeal before the judgment is entered or after judgment has been entered, but while a timely filed tolling motion is pending but not yet decided by the trial court. What happens then?

As you now understand, the general rule is such notices of appeal become effective without further action once the appealable event occurs.

For example, under the federal rules of appellate procedure, a notice of appeal filed "after the court announces a decision or order—but before entry of the judgment or order—is treated as filed on the date of and after the entry."[46] This renders a premature notice perfected when the docket entry or judgment is filed. It is always wise to file another notice of appeal after the judgment is docketed.

It is important to note and understand the qualifier in this sentence—the notice of appeal must be filed *after the court announces a decision or order.*

More importantly, the "decision or order" referred to in the rule must be a decision or order appealable once the entry requirements are met. If the requirements are not met, then the notice of appeal is premature and is null and void.

PRACTICE POINTER

File multiple notice of appeals if and when there is uncertainty as to the effective date of the judgment and/or docket entry.

Some, but not all, state courts are willing to hear a case despite a premature notice of appeal, but where hearing an appeal depends on the exercise of discretion, there is a limit to the appellate court's procedural patience.

Q. NOTICES OF APPEAL AFTER JUDGMENT OR DOCKET ENTRY

A notice of appeal filed after entry of judgment, but while a "tolling motion" is pending, is likely ineffective. Thus you must file a new or amended notice of appeal. And that is the key.

---

46. Federal Rules of Appellate Procedure Rule 4(a)(2).

If you file motions tolling the time to file a notice of appeal, you simply file a new notice appeal, or a notice of appeal in a timely manner, after the trial court dockets the decision on your or the other party's motions.

R. WHAT IF YOU MISS THE DEADLINE?

What happens when you fail to file the notice of appeal within thirty days of the judgment being entered upon the docket?

Generally, no relief as a matter of right is available from the late filing of a notice of appeal. This is due to the jurisdictional nature of the appeals court. If a deadline is missed, then it precludes the appeals court from taking jurisdiction over the matter.

There are very limited circumstances when both federal and state courts permit discretionary authority to allow a court to extend the time to file a notice of appeal. These rules tend to be wholly discretionary and are usually subject to further appellate review, if you proceed under a late filing local rule.

In California, a court lacks authority to extend or modify the time to file a notice of appeal.[47] Late filing of the notice of appeal results in dismissal of the appeal on the merits.

Some states allow for an additional extension of time. For example, Hawaii, Indiana, New Mexico, Rhode Island, and Utah allow discretion in allowing a late notice of appeal filing.

Other states allow filing a notice of an appeal upon a showing of excusable neglect. Massachusetts is an example.[48] The lower court has discretionary power to extend the time for filing the notice of appeal for any party for an additional thirty-day period.[49]

Finally, some states afford a litigant extraordinary relief by asking the appeals to allow a late notice within one (1) year of the entry of the judgment.[50] This requires a filing of a motion with the appel-

47. Eisenberg, Horvitz & Weiner, California Practice Guide—Civil Appeals and Writs § 2:13 (Rutter, rev, 2009) (emphasis in text).

48. Massachusetts Rules of Appellate Procedure Rule 4.

49. *Id.*

50. *Id.*

late court. The appellate court is afforded discretion to grant or not grant your motion. A compelling reason is necessary. For example, your client needs time to raise funds to prosecute his or her appeal.

S. CROSS APPEALS ("MULTIPLE APPEALS")

Sometimes your opponent may appeal at the same time you filed your notice or after you have both filed notice of appeals.

In that event, there is what are sometimes called "cross-appeals," or what rule 4(a)(3) of the Federal Rules of Appellate Procedure calls "multiple appeals."

Special timing rules for more than one appeal in an action are necessary to prevent "sandbagging." This is because your client might be content to allow a judgment to become final without pursuing an appeal until such time as his wife suddenly seeks appellate redress.

If your opponent, the wife, however, filed her notice of appeal on the very last day allotted by the time proscribed local rule, then in the absence of any special rules, it would be too late for your client, the husband, to reconsider his original choice to not appeal.

To avoid such a scenario, appellate rules universally provide additional time for the filing of a second notice of appeal following the filing of the first notice. Your husband client therefore receives a second chance to seek his appeal.

Under the Federal Rules of Appellate Procedure, for example, a party has fourteen (14) days from the filing of the first notice of appeal and most states afford a similar or slightly larger amount of time.[51]

T. KNOW WHEN TO APPEAL

There are wide variations among the states in the handling of when to appeal an order of the trial court. For example, New York allows for almost all orders to be reviewed to a higher court.

51. Federal Rules of Appellate Procedure Rule 4.

While in West Virginia, there is a more restrictive approach. There is no right of appeal in civil cases. Rather, a party seeking to appeal must petition to the West Virginia Supreme Court of Appeals for the right to proceed.[52]

Over in Oklahoma, all civil appeals are initially filed with the Oklahoma Supreme Court. The high court in Oklahoma then assigns the matter to the Oklahoma Court of Appeals unless they grant a party's right to have the case heard by the Oklahoma Supreme Court.[53]

Utah is similar to Oklahoma, as its supreme court technically has appellate jurisdiction over all civil appeals, but with the exception of certain matters over which the court has exclusive jurisdiction, civil appeals automatically "pour over" to the courts of appeal unless a party successfully asks the Utah Supreme Court to retain jurisdiction.[54]

The bottom line is to know and understand the proper filing of a notice of appeal and the time constraints required by your local rules, including the effect of post-trial motions upon the notice of appeal. Once the notice is proper and effective, we can next turn to ensuring the appellate court receives what is needed to evaluate the merits of your appeal.

52. West Virginia Rules of Appellate Procedure, Rules 3 and 7.
53. Oklahoma Supreme Court Rules 1.23 and 1.24.
54. Utah State Legislature, § 78A-3-102(4).

8 How to Assemble the Record, Correct Errors, Protect Confidential Information, and Docket the Appeal

When you appeal, it is your responsibility to ensure the record is assembled and presented to the appellate court for review. The trial court is responsible for the assembly of the record itself, but the burden is on you to ensure the record is properly filed with the appeals court. For example, trial transcripts may be required and it may be your burden to pay for those transcripts and have these filed with the trial court as part of the court's assembly of the record.

The record on an appeal consists of every original document contained within the file of the lower clerk as certified by the trial court's clerk. This should include all pleadings, all exhibits at trial, and items such as financial statements or third-party reports. The record includes the actual docket entries of the matter maintained by the trial court clerk. In essence, what we mean by the record is everything submitted to the lower court, not just the items submitted at trial.

But keep in mind everything in the trial court record is not necessarily part of the appellate record in a practical sense or even under the local rules adopted in a particular appeals court. This is an important distinction for you to understand as you prepare your appeal.

The record *in practice* are those documents presented before the appeals court for review. These documents are generally found within the Record Appendix presented to the reviewing court.

The Record Appendix is part of your brief or the materials *you submit* to the appeals court with your brief when it is filed. It is not the larger record itself. Therefore, the record actually "reviewed" is in reality your own Record Appendix.

PRACTICE POINTER

Understand the difference between the record of the court and record appendix, which you create to support your brief and submit to the court along with your brief.

A. THE DUTIES WHEN YOU ARE THE APPELLANT

When you are representing an appellant, you are responsible to ensure the lower court transmits the trial record to the appeals court. No, this does not mean you need to rent a pickup truck to deliver the record from the trial court to the steps of the appeals court.

Rather, as a matter of practice, a member of the lower court clerk's office—one who is specially designated to handle appeals—is responsible for identifying the physical files and preparing them for shipment to the appeals court upon notice that the matter is being appealed to the higher court.

For example, pursuant to the federal rules, the district court clerk must "number the documents constituting the record and send them promptly to the circuit clerk together with a list of the documents correspondingly numbered and reasonably identified."[55]

55. Federal Rules of Appellate Procedure Rule 11(b)(2).

In practice in the federal court, the district court clerk transmits everything except those items specifically excluded under the Federal Rules of Appellate Procedure or Local Rules. This is generally those items too heavy for transport or transcripts not designated for the appeal.

Keep in mind that trial courts exclude certain materials from the transmission of local court files, such as briefs, notices, subpoenas, summonses, or affidavits of service. You therefore may need to demonstrate that the material is relevant to your appeal.

In a family law matter, the trial court is unlikely to include financial statements and/or Guardian ad litem reports, which are kept separate from the regular court file for confidentiality reasons. Include these important records within your Record Appendix. Or, ask that they be filed under seal with the court of appeals.

The local court clerk's duty to transmit the record commences when the record is deemed complete and when all pertinent transcripts are filed.

B. TRIAL TRANSCRIPTS

When you are representing the appellant, it is your obligation to ensure all transcripts are filed with the trial court. Be familiar with your local rules to ensure the transcripts confirm with any required rules of the appellate court. For example, some appellate courts require the transcriber to be certified by the appeals court or to follow a certain appellate format.

PRACTICE POINTER

A stenographer hired for trial can ensure a complete and thorough record.

Notify the trial court when the transcripts are completed and the record is "assembled."

A written letter stating the record is complete is sufficient. Thereafter, the trial court's clerk notifies the parties and the clerk transmits the complete record to the appeals court.

C. STRATEGIC CONSIDERATIONS

Transcripts are critical in any appeal for both sides. Transcripts may directly reveal the judge's errors, but likewise demonstrate the absence of any trial errors. They are critical for both parties.

The importance of transcripts in family law matter can flow beyond trial transcripts to pretrial proceedings. Even if some transcripts are not required to address the issues on appeal, review transcripts of pretrial proceedings and even motion hearings. You may just find yourself striking gold by reviewing the entirety of the matter.

Take the example of a motion hearing, which results in an award of "temporary custody" of the parties' only child to the opponent party.

Motion hearings are not "per se evidentiary events." In other words, there is no testimony or evidence, only the arguments of respective counsel for the parties.

This brings to mind the old family law joke: domestic relations is the only area of the law where parties argue and lawyers testify.

Anyway, perhaps your lawyer-opponent makes a critical misrepresentation in his argument to the trial judge. For example, he asserts the father does drugs.

It later turns out the representation is untrue and the trial judge was in error to award temporary custody based only upon the lawyer's false representation.

Obtain the transcript of the temporary order hearing in question and include it within your Record Appendix even though it is not trial testimony. It demonstrates the potential error from the inception of the trial and allows you to argue it within your brief.

D. IMPORTANCE OF TRANSCRIPTS

Further, transcripts are critical, as they can provide a window into the whole of the trial court proceedings. They can grab a reader's attention in a way a brief may not.

If you were not trial counsel, transcripts provide you with useful context, permitting you a better understanding of what occurred at trial. The primary example would be of a custody matter where the trial judge did seem favorable to your client. Perhaps a single nugget read in the transcript provides you with the reason why.

Reading trial and record transcripts is also excellent preparation for your oral argument. It is your responsibility to become an expert on the record on appeal and what happened below

PRACTICE POINTER

Always read each and every word of the trial transcript even if you were trial counsel.

Always order a trial transcript where one of your arguments is that the findings of fact are not supported by the evidence submitted. Provide the reviewing court with all of the evidence supporting the findings, including all transcribed testimony related to the finding of fact being challenged. This requires you to designate numerous transcripts for inclusion in your Record Appendix.

In contrast, some appeals present you with scant trial testimony or narrow issues for appellate court review. On those occasions, you do not need testimony or hearing transcripts to submit to the reviewing court.

Take the example of a matter to be submitted to the trial court *by representation only*, if and when allowed by your local rules. In this situation, there is no testimony, only argument by counsel. A transcript may not be necessary or needed. Regardless, obtain the transcript of the argument by your representation.

One appellate caveat of which to be aware: arguments by representation, without testimony of parties or witnesses, are universally appellate traps leading to remand.

Without trial testimony, the reviewing court lacks factual evidence to properly review the matter. This often results in the matter being remanded to the trial judge when the matter is appealed for further evidence. You end up back to where you began.

Further, many times arguments by representation only result in the trial judge relying upon *parole evidence* to make a decision.

This is ripe ground for the appellant to argue and can likely result in the matter to be remanded.

A consideration for any argument to be made by representation only, which can be cost-effective, is to state that any decision is nonappealable absent fraud or extraordinary circumstances.

E. DOCUMENTS

Ensure all documents submitted to the lower court (exhibits, financial statements, etc.) are part of the actual record submitted to the appeals court.

F. TRANSCRIPT DELAYS

Be prepared to identify transcript-related problems early in the appellate process and work cooperatively with your opponent to resolve them. Delays happen to you and do happen often. You may find you are better served by working collaboratively with your opponent's counsel to rectify transcript issues.

Explain to your client that delays in the preparation of transcripts can add several months to the duration of an appeal. Clients must be informed of the cost of transcription.

As discussed, but worth a reminder, always prepare your client for the probability of delays in the preparation of transcripts, and consider the time element with him or her as part of the decision to appeal. The cost must be included in this discussion.

Always keep your client informed of the status of the preparation of the transcripts necessary to be filed as part of the record on appeal.

G. CORRECTING THE RECORD

What happens when there are issues with errors or omissions contained within the record? For example, the trial transcript is missing pages or parts of testimony went unrecorded, thereby making it impossible to transcribe.

Both the federal rules and state rules establish procedures for correcting the record even when the parties disagree to what transpired in the trial court. The broad nature of these rules allows you to correct an issue related to the record. Seek relief for your client when you believe something material to the appeal is missing from the record or is inaccurate.[56]

Among possible factors to allege in a motion seeking to suspend the rules for good cause are (1) no other available remedies to resolve the problem and (2) the interest of justice is served by granting the relief you are seeking.

An example is if the recording is inaccurate or unintelligible.[57] Even though a Federal Rule 10(e)(1) or a Federal Rule 10 (e)(2) motion may overlap to cover many of the same problems with a record, there is one important difference: A Rule 10(e)(1) motion (or your local rules equivalent) is presented to the trial court.

In contrast, a Rule 10(e)(2) motion (or your local rules equivalent) addressing materials erroneously omitted or misstated in the record provides you with the choice of seeking relief from either the trial court or the appellate court.

You may also seek relief under the catchall provision found in Federal Rule 10(e)(3) (or your local rules equivalent).

Or:

Seek to resolve the issue by an agreement with your opposing counsel.

You may encounter mistakes contained in the production of the transcript. It is best practice to always attempt to correct such errors upon receiving the transcript, but such timely changes often do not occur in practice.

Often, time is short and the transcript needs to be filed to continue to process your appeal.

If you identify a mistake or error in the transcription, then it is your job to determine how to resolve such errors contained in the record. It is incumbent upon you to move under your local applicable rule for relief from the error contained within the transcription.

---

56. Federal Rule of Appellate Procedure Rule 10(e)(2).
57. Federal Rule of Appellate Procedure Rule 10(e)(1).

Further, your potential failure to do so may result in a waiver of the claimed inaccuracy in the record.

H. SO HOW DO YOU HANDLE?

What do you do when you encounter a situation where it is important to supplement the trial record?

The Ninth Circuit Court of Appeals addressed the requirements for supplementing the record on appeal in the unusual context of one enterprising lawyer who attempted to sue the judge who continually ruled against him.[58]

The attorney attempted to have the judge investigated and disqualified from the attorney's future cases and to require the Social Security Administration (SSA) where he appeared to promulgate final procedures for bias complaints.

Although the ninth circuit rejected the creative attorney's claims, it cautioned and sanctioned the SSA for improperly bringing in extra-record material on appeal.

The SSA submitted, along with its brief, a "Supplemental Excerpts of Record," which consisted of a letter from another administrative law judge to the attorney. But this letter was not part of the record contained in the lower court. In fact, it actually postdated the notice of appeal and even the appellant's opening brief.

The ninth circuit held that parties may not unilaterally supplement the record with evidence not contained within in the actual trial record, as it would be unfair to the court and to the opposing party. This is the established rule in every jurisdiction.

The proper way to address "after-the-fact evidence" is to file a motion in the court of appeals. Your motion would either result in a remand to the trial court for further fact-finding or the court of appeals would instruct you the evidence comes far too late in the game for any consideration.

In family law, matters occurring postjudgment result in grounds for a modification action rather than a reopening of the record for additional evidence.

58. Lowry v. Barnhart, 329 F.3d 1019, 1020 (9th Cir. 2003).

Take the father who has custody of the parties' children, but postjudgment develops a rather nasty alcohol problem.

The proper procedure is to seek relief ***to change, not challenge the judgment*** with this new event. Thus it would be proper to file modification in the lower court and not attempt to expand the applicable record with a new postjudgment event.

PRACTICE POINTER

Understand and acknowledge the difference between challenging a judgment and changing a judgment.

However, if the matter is pending before the appeals court during the time the new events of the father's troubling drinking occurs, file a motion with the appeals court for permission to move forward with the modification action in the lower court, as the appellate court has jurisdiction during the pendency of the appeal.

In addition, most modification actions limit evidence to those events from the prior judgment forward and not from past events prior to the judgment, under the doctrine of issue preclusion and or res judicata.

Conversely, family law appeals are limited to events of the judgment on appeal and the evidence resulting in that judgment *only*.

In the non-family law example above, what the SSA did was simply thrust the evidence before the court of appeals. The appeals court does not look kindly on a party taking unilateral action without permission and you should avoid it and utilize the proper procedure when faced with this type of dilemma by filing an appropriate motion to supplement the record. If not, you run the risk of being hit with monetary sanctions.

I. CONFIDENTIAL INFORMATION

Most family law appeals contain confidential information. As a result, your assembly of the record and your Record Appendix will likely contain confidential material. This confidential information is segregated from the record you submit to the reviewing court. For example, you submit two Record Appendixes, one of which is labeled for confidential information only.

Consult local rules to determine the specific type of information to segregate from the material you assembled as part of the record.

State rules differ, but generally documents requiring protection from the public record are financial statements, exhibits containing social security numbers, state and federal tax returns, W-2s, retirement statements, bank statements, credit card statements, Guardian ad litem reports, and/or probation reports.

PRACTICE POINTER

It is very likely your appeal contains confidential information requiring segregation from other information contained in your brief.

J. DESIGNATE CONFIDENTIAL INFORMATION

Designate confidential information cited in your brief during your drafting. Prepare a separate Record Appendix for this protected information. By doing so from the beginning, you avoid removing this confidential information from the publicly available Record Appendix at the last minute.

There is no worse feeling than realizing you cited confidential information in your Record Appendix and it needs to be segregated into a separate Record Appendix at the last minute. The Record Appendix is discussed in greater detail in the next chapter.

This duty to protect confidential materials rests with you always and not with any court. In general, confidentiality rules require the following:[59]

1. **The parties refrain from disclosing impounded material, unless necessary.**

   Again, courts place the burden upon you from disclosing protected information.

59. From the Massachusetts Supreme Judicial Court Rule 1:24: Protection of personal identifying information in publicly accessible court documents.

2. **The disclosing party, when disclosure is absolutely necessary, should file and serve a written notice of the disclosure or filing of such information.**

   There may be times when you wish to disclose confidential information to make your case. Provide notice and seek permission to prevent violating your duty to disclose. Again, proceed with caution.
3. **The cover of briefs, record appendices, and other filings containing impounded material clearly indicate its inclusion (e.g., "Impounded" or "Contains references to impounded material").**

   This is a common error of your brother and sister appellate counsel. They fail to denote that a separate Record Appendix contains impounded information.

   For example, in a child custody matter, you include in the Record Appendix the Guardian ad litem report and cite it throughout your brief and attach it at the end of the Record Appendix without designating on the cover it contains "impounded material." This is improper.

   Instead create a separate Record Appendix for protected information.
4. **In cases where only certain portions of the record need to be impounded, parties file a separate Record Appendix volume containing only that material, with its cover labeled as containing impounded material.**
5. **The parties use a pseudonym or initials if a party's name is confidential or impounded.**

   This is always good practice even when the material is not impounded.
6. **A copy of any order of impoundment shall be included in the Record Appendix.**

   Always include impoundment orders. It ensures the appellate court record has them and demonstrates you are careful and trustworthy with confidential information. Your good sense builds credibility with the appellate court.
7. **The parties must not disclose impounded material at oral argument unless necessary and, in such instances, must notify the clerk in advance and, in appropriate cases, make such disclosures in a manner protecting the confidential information.**

Your duty to protect impounded material does not stop at your brief and creation of the Record Appendix, but continues to your oral argument.

If you get into the habit of protecting confidential information, it carries through to when you are facing your appellate panel at oral argument. Your care avoids any unintended slipups under the pressure of oral argument.

Use the following three fundamental rules to assist you in your use of confidential information in your preparation of the record. But always read your local rules to ensure compliance with rules of privacy and confidentiality.

RULE 1 "Use Extreme Caution in Protecting Confidential Information in the Record, the Brief, and Your Record Appendix"

Be overly protective of any potential confidential information.

When there is any doubt as to the status of the information, choose to protect it; for example, a document containing information both confidential and nonconfidential. It is better to seek protection of the document for three reasons:

First, it is your duty to protect the confidential information. Second, it is good practice when dealing with family law matters to exercise extreme caution due to the intimate nature of the issues and emotions of the parties involved. And third, it is better for an appellate court to reject your good sense than for the court to bounce your submissions for failing to do so.

RULE 2 "Avoid the Name of Children or Party Names in Your Brief"

You want to provide a personal and/or more intimate slant within your brief, but use caution against using children or party names within your brief.

Here is why.

First, it incites the other side in a matter that is already a "powder keg" by the time you reach the appellate court. Second, it makes no difference in your brief. The law is the law. The analysis remains the analysis. There is no bang for the buck here. And third, you may run up against local rules prohibiting using a child's name within your brief.

RULE 3 "Always Protect Personal Identifying Information (PII)"

Always protect personal identifying information (PII) when filing any publicly accessible court document. Most states and federal rules now require you to protect this type of information.

PII includes a party's social security number, taxpayer identification number, driver's license number, state-issued ID card number, passport number, any financial account numbers, any credit or debit card numbers, and parents' birth surnames. Always have your guard up when you are confronted with the use of this information.

The general rule of protecting PII is applicable to publicly accessible documents such as briefs, appendices, motions, or really any other filings accessible to the public.

So what happens when you are confronted with this material?

For example, you want to include credit card statements ignored by the trial in your Record Appendix. Be sure to redact the statements to comply with local rules concerning PII.

The general rule of redaction is to redact PII in documents by replacing the omitted information with the use of "xxx" or "beginning/ending with." For example, state your client's driver's license number ending with "23" or a party checking account ending in "xxx645."

PRACTICE POINTER

Redact when you have any concern with the use of confidential information.

Use strong black pen and with a strong hand. Ensure your same strong hand makes all redactions properly to prevent anyone from being able to find the PII. For example, ensure the material is no longer visible.

What do you do when you want to utilize unredacted information in your brief or Record Appendix?

In those situations, first obtain the leave of the appeals court and demonstrate a compelling reason to use such information.

K. DOCKETING THE APPEAL

1. Filing Fees

Upon the assembly of the record in the lower court, most states require you *to enter* the matter in the appropriate appeals court and to pay the applicable required filing fee.

Always inform your client there is a court-administered fee for any party appealing any aspect of the judgment. Once again, consult your local rules to determine the cost of filing the appeal.

After notification that the record is assembled, the appeals court allows you a short period of time to pay the required fee and then the matter is entered on the appellate docket.

L. INDIGENT CLIENTS

What if your client is indigent?

Take the example of representing a client pro bono who qualifies as indigent. Always first review local rules for waiver of any required fees and identify any available resources for indigent parties.

Appellate courts waive the docket fee for indigent parties. A motion accompanied with a financial affidavit is required to be submitted to waive the applicable appellate court fee at the time of docketing the appeal.

Check to see if there are any resources available for the cost of submissions, including transcripts.

Further, if it is possible in your matter, file a request for appellate fees with your trial judge. This motion should be filed upon receiving the notice of appeal and while the trial court retains jurisdiction over the matter before it is entered in the appellate court.

In the event the matter is within the appellate court's jurisdiction, then seek leave from the appellate court to file your motion for fees to prosecute the appeal in the trial court.

M. DOCKETING STATEMENT

Most states require a docketing statement. This filing is generally filed at the time of perfecting the appeal or soon thereafter, depending on your local rules.

Some jurisdictions require filing the docketing statement when the notice of appeal is presented to the trial court. Other jurisdictions require filing after the appeal is docketed within the appeals court.

Appeals courts nationwide adopted these statements to more efficiently and expeditiously administer the crowded judicial appellate calendar. Pay attention to this requirement, as a failure to file can result in the dismissal of the appeal. In contrast to the notice of appeal, the docketing statement is not a jurisdictional document requirement. It is utilized for internal court procedure and is administrative in nature.

Here is an example.

Pennsylvania requires an appealing party to send a docketing statement form to be completed and returned within ten (10) days of the matter being entered in the appellate court.[60]

The requirements of docketing statements can vary but include the following:

1. A statement identifying the parties
2. A jurisdictional statement
3. A mini-description of the case to be appealed
4. Information regarding the record or transcripts
5. Any other information that may be requested by your local appellate court to assist in administration of the court

Now that you have ensured the record is assembled properly and filed the required fees and your case is properly docketed within the appeals court, it is time to get started on preparing to draft your appellate brief by first creating the critical Record Appendix.

60. 210 Pennsylvania Code Rule 3517.

9 The Importance of the Record Appendix

The Record Appendix is different than the "record" the trial court transfers to the appeals court. It is those documents you are asking the appeals court to review in connection with your own argument and not everything contained within the court file.

The Record Appendix contents vary by rule. For example, in Massachusetts, the rule is the appendix is "the collection of those portions of the trial court's record (e.g., papers, exhibits and/or transcripts) relevant to the issues, facts, and arguments set forth in your brief."[61] The rule requires "a copy of the trial court docket, as well as a copy of the order, judgment, or decree being appealed."[62]

It is your responsibility to bring before the appellate court any document and/or transcript necessary to decide your appeal. If you do not include a document, then the court of appeals does not consider it.

61. Massachusetts Rules of Appellate Procedure Rule 18.
62. *Id.*

Only include parts of the trial court record you deem relevant to overturning or sustaining the judgment entered by the trial court.

Develop what evidence to utilize from the beginning of your handling of the appeal.

Use the Record Appendix as a road map of your appeal.

In theory, trial court material not contained in the Record Appendix is available to the appellate court from the complete record itself supplied from the clerk of the trial court. But the focus of the Record Appendix must be upon each and every document necessary to make your argument.

Never rely on the appeals court searching for documents within the larger record. Rather, the appellate court relies on your Record Appendix.

It is therefore important to distinguish between the trial record maintained by the lower court and all the materials included in your Record Appendix.

Your failure to distinguish between the trial record and your Record Appendix can lead to making mistakes. The most common potential error to avoid is thinking evidence is properly before the appellate court when it is not.

How can this happen?

Any time a Record Appendix[63] does not contain the entire trial court record there will be trial court material which is not easily available for review by the appellate court. Some courts only review what you present in the Record Appendix.

As a result, if your appeal points to a critical document that was left out of the Record Appendix but was contained in the trial record, it may never be examined by the appellate court.

Understand how your appellate court handles the trial court's formal record and whether it is actually reviewed in your appeal. Review your local rules and check with a local appeals court clerk.

Some appellate courts use different terms to refer to what is meant by the Record Appendix (RA). But the *Record Appendix* or sometimes *appendix* is the most common term.

---

63. Record Appendix (RA). Keep in mind the Record Appendix is capitalized to distinguish your understanding from the record.

A. STRATEGY

There is a balancing act of being either under-inclusive or over-inclusive when designating material for your Record Appendix.

Use all relevant material to support your client's argument.

But what about negative evidence against your client?

There are times when your client's interests may not always be furthered by bringing all material into the Record Appendix. On those occasions, limit your material to only what makes your client's case.

But a note of extreme caution.

If you leave a glaring omission from the RA, the reviewing court may find your submission lacks integrity, particularly when the evidence is material to the issues on appeal.

For example, perhaps you are arguing the lower court abused its discretion by awarding custody to the opposing party without sufficient evidence. But you did not include in your Record Appendix the guardian ad litem report, which provided the critical findings the trial judge relied upon.

This failure to include this critical evidence in your Record Appendix is an example of a glaring omission. The appellate court will notice your failure to include this pertinent exhibit.

You never want to lose credibility. Each submission counts. You are better served by addressing and attacking an opponent's unfavorable evidence to your client.

B. REQUIREMENTS OF A JOINT APPENDIX

States require parties to submit a joint appendix or rather require you to attempt to do so.

A single appendix is favored by the appellate court. It saves the appellate court the time going back and forth between multiple Record Appendixes.

However, in practice, a joint RA requires cooperation with your opponent. This is often less than ideal by the time you reach the appellate stage. Further, appellate courts require you to resolve any "appendix disputes" by counsel.

One advantage to filing a joint Record Appendix is to share the substantial costs of preparation with your opponent. Always something to consider for your client.

C. SUPPLEMENTAL RECORD APPENDIX

The appellant prepares the Record Appendix. But what happens when you represent the appellee and you are not satisfied with the Record Appendix?

For example, the Record Appendix of the appellant is missing a key pretrial ruling favorable for your client.

When you represent the appellee, seek to supplement the Record Appendix with your own new material from the record. This is accomplished by filing a routine motion to file a Supplemental Record Appendix.

D. WHAT IS THE CONTENT AND FORM OF A JOINT APPENDIX?

The content and form of the appendix are dictated by local rules. Here are some examples.

In Maryland, the rule is to include "all parts of the record that are reasonably necessary" to decide the appeal and, indeed, now encompasses "any cross-appeal."[64]

The Federal Rule 30(a)(1) requires the appellant to include the following items in the appendix:

1. Docket sheet with relevant entries
2. Relevant portions of the pleadings
3. Jury charge and lower court's opinion or findings
4. The judgment, order, or decision being appealed
5. And any "other parts of the record to which the parties wish to direct the court's attention."[65]

---

64. Maryland Rule of Appellate Practice Rule 8-501(c).
65. Federal Rules of Appellate Procedure Rule 30(a)(1)(A)–(D).

The Record Appendix consists of a table of contents, any relevant docket entries, and then all other parts you reference in your brief in chronological order.

Your job is to make the RA reader-friendly so you may avoid duplicate exhibits.

Your failure to comply with the applicable rules and requirements of the Record Appendix can lead to having to refile a new one or even dismissal of your client's appeal.

Pay close attention to your local rules.

PRACTICE POINTER

Think of the record appendix as your offer of proof to the appeals court and it is comprised of materials necessary to correct the wrong of the lower court.

E. WHAT SHOULD GO IN?

Include all relevant material necessary to determine your issues on appeal, while not overwhelming the court with any unnecessary or superfluous information.

Be diligent in your selection of the material and use it to enhance your brief—as it is the support for the arguments you are making before the appeals court.

Outline both your major and minor points first and then search for the evidentiary support in the record to support your arguments.

Start with the major points. Identify the key ingredients supporting your argument.

For example, if the major issues are financial, seek out the important financial information submitted to the lower court. Utilize the critical financial documents only: financial statements, tax returns, or offers of employment.

Pull those out and include them within your Record Appendix.

For key documents, include the entirety of the evidence to provide the appellate court with a complete understanding.

But do not feel compelled to be duplicative.

If there are five financial statements, then use only the trial financial affidavit to make your point.

Then review the more minor points.

Issues may need to be covered, but in far less detail in your brief and with far less evidentiary support. Find items and material to support those less contested propositions and include those evidentiary components within the Record Appendix.

PRACTICE POINTER

Create your own appendix of documents, testimony, or evidence you want the appellate court to review and then ensure it is within the record the appeals court is actually reviewing.

Follow the default rule, "If in doubt, don't leave it out," in your assembly of the record. But likewise, if you are the appellee and need additional items not included by the appellant, then file a Supplemental Record Appendix.

The general rule is any gap you leave in the appellate record counts against your client. Even worse, when you fail to provide to the appeals court a sufficient record, the court may choose to decline to consider the issue you argued in your brief.

In addition, there is nothing more embarrassing than being before an appellate panel in oral argument and trying to state a document exists in the record when it does not.

Here is an example.

Issues with the record were a major problem in the appeal involving former Los Angeles Clippers owner Donald Sterling.[66]

Mr. Sterling attempted to regain ownership of the Clippers from former Microsoft chief executive officer, Steve Ballmer, by arguing he was improperly removed as one of the team's owners.

The California Court of Appeal rejected his appeal, noting a number of problems with his appeal, which included factual claims

66. Sterling v. Sterling, 242 Cal. App. 4th 185, 194–195 (2015).

without record citation and using quoted material without identifying the volume and page number in the record.

When you are the appellant, always take particular care in preparing the Record Appendix. It is your ultimate responsibility. This includes those times when you and your opposing counsel can agree on a joint filing.

In summary, do not underestimate the importance of creating a good Record Appendix from the beginning of your representation of your client. A Record Appendix serves as an important road map to support your argument. It is the collective evidence shining the light upon your legal reasoning. Use it to your advantage to stay organized during your representation of your client.

Once you have created your Record Appendix containing all pertinent material to demonstrate the logic and the power of your argument, it is time to start preparing to write the brief.

10 Preparing to Write the Brief: Outline, Theme, Style, Using Authorities, Effective Techniques, and Drafting Considerations

A. OUTLINE

Your overall objective in writing a brief is to make the job easy for the appellate court. Proper organization prior to your brief drafting improves the quality of your submission to the reviewing court. Some fundamentals are essential to ensure the end result is a product worthy of the argument you are making.

Utilize your own organizational style to formulate your brief. It is your "voice" and your style that dictates how it is ultimately written. But as you draft, keep in mind the overall objective is ease of argument.

Prepare a framework to present the "best" arguments in your most persuasive manner. An outline is a critical first step in helping you formulate your thoughts and an excellent place for you to begin your drafting.

In the same way a builder relies on an architect's drawing, use a preliminary outline to organize your thoughts and ideas.

The outline serves as your guide for drafting your brief. If you have been paying attention, you have been preparing to outline your brief from the commencement of the action.

Begin your outline by sorting out the major issues according to priority. Identify and stay focused upon your "best" arguments for review and potential remand or reversal.

Then select all other major issues to be challenged on appeal.

Let's take an alimony example.

Take where your client has been "hit" with an alimony judgment misapplying his income by a significant portion due to a one-time financial positive event, such as receiving an incentive bonus. In addition, the same alimony order fails to consider the wife's part-time income.

Here are two major issues you are challenging on appeal:

a. **The determination of the husband's income**
b. **The lack of consideration of the wife's income**

Each of these issues provides you with a general category to build your argument.

For example, under each issue category, A and B, provide all relevant support for your brief. Go further by breaking down supportive information into subtopics, such as evidence, case citations, and the applicable standard of review under each issue category.

Here is an example of how to outline the two major issues.

I. **THE DETERMINATION OF THE HUSBAND'S INCOME**

EVIDENCE

A. Page 7 of the judgment ignores the husband's last two years of income.
B. Page 227 of the husband's testimony discusses the one-time event that led to higher income.
C. Page 323 Exhibit is husband's compensation plan.

LAW

D. Alimony Statute of the State of Utopia specifically allows for discretion in the exclusion of some one-time events for purposes of compensation for ongoing alimony awards.

II. THE LACK OF CONSIDERATION OF THE WIFE'S INCOME

EVIDENCE

A. Page 17 of the judgment ignores the wife's income in the calculation of alimony.

B. Page 96 of the record lists the wife's income on her financial affidavit.

C. Page 298 of the wife's trial testimony discusses her job and salary as a part-time nurse.

LAW

D. Alimony Statute specifically states part-time income should be considered in the determination of an alimony award.

As you draft your outline, add case law and statutory references and start to connect them to the facts heard during the trial. Think connect the dots in your logic.

Remain flexible with your outline and delete information not supporting your argument. Many times, your initial outline is too overbroad.

Focus on articulating only salient and critical matters requiring judicial intervention from above. To use a hockey analogy, think "major" penalties not "minor" infractions.

Finally, consider and brief the applicable standard of review.

The determination of the standard of review is an important analysis and the answer is not always clear from the outset of your case. You may even change the standard of review when you begin drafting your brief.

Take again our alimony example above.

The appropriate standard of review is either an abuse of discretion—the failure to account for both the one-time event and the wife's part-time job—or an error of law by not including the statutorily required "all income of the parties."

Practice Pointer

Always start with an outline of the major issues to be challenged, but be flexible to add or alter your outline as you draft.

In short, your outline brings attention to what is *truly important* to argue in your brief.

B. THEME

Develop your theme early in your preparation. It serves as a lighthouse to remind you of the purpose of your argument. Think of it as your "hook."

You want to promptly get "to the heart of the matter" in any written legal argument. Judges lack patience and your job is to lead early and often with your best appellate punch.

Isolate the main issue, explain its importance, and state the necessary solution. This approach begins with the theme of the case.

Start by drafting a summary paragraph, which can later be placed within the body of your argument. Include the summary within your outline.

Here is an example:

> The lower court's decision to award custody of Jacob to his mother raises a single issue: Did the court award custody based only upon the report of the guardian ad litem (GAL) and not based upon the weight of the evidence submitted at trial as required by *Roberta v. Roberta,* 923 Utopia 549 (1995)? The lower court abused its discretion in its custodial award of Jacob by not weighing the evidence and relying solely upon the GAL report as is required by *Shapiro v. Ganz,* 109 Utopia 164 (1999).

> The matter should be returned to the lower court to weigh the evidence along with the guardian ad litem report to determine custody of Jacob.

This summary succinctly provides the reader with the essential problem: the judge relied only upon the GAL report and not with any necessary independent evidence. This example provides the controlling authorities and the context, specifies the standard of review, and advises the appellate court of your proposed solution. Return to your theme again as you develop your argument further. Utilize it when you prepare for oral argument. You can also apply this same skill to your trials to allow you to quote from it in your summary of facts on appeal.

PRACTICE POINTER

Always develop your theme early and add it to the outline of your brief.

C. STYLE

All effective written arguments possess certain common characteristics. Appeals court readers look for styles they are accustomed to. There are five common elements in all impactful written briefs.

Incorporate these five fundamental elements to ensure your brief rings familiar with your appellate readers. First, as discussed above, always identify your argument's theme in the beginning of your brief.

Second, focus only on critical arguments in a concise manner.

Third, use the facts in your case to frame your legal arguments. This allows you to build your legal arguments upon the important factual landscape. Strive to have your brief readers nodding their head as they read along.

Fourth, identify up front the major legal precedents and/or statutes presented in your case. There may be multiple angles to play, but play your strongest hand with the law in play.

Finally, apply your facts to the controlling case law to demonstrate how your facts support your argument. If your case differs from current controlling legal precedent, then use the opportunity to demonstrate how and why.

D. CONTEXT AND AUTHORITIES

Set the stage for your legal arguments by placing the facts in proper content in the law. By doing so, the appellate court receives the necessary background to which the authorities must then be applied. More importantly, the appellate court receives a greater understanding of the happenings at trial.

Setting a proper perspective is important because the facts are the "human element" of appellate review. Matters are real. Remind the appellate court of the breathing and living issues by your use of the events involved.

Here is an example.

The trial court is considering which parent should be awarded custody of the parties' children.

A guardian ad litem report is submitted recommending custody be awarded to the mother.

The father offers the following evidence in support of his request for custody and the lower court ignores the following:

1. The father stayed home with both children for the past twelve years.
2. The father was the only parent who arranged the children's schedule.
3. The father was the only parent who took the children to all of their doctor appointments.
4. The father was the only parent who went to the children's parent-teacher conferences.

All four of the above critical facts demonstrate that the trial court ignored important evidence of the father's substantial parenting role. You set the stage with these critical four facts to thereafter weave the applicable law into your argument. For example, the argument is the trial judge did not properly weigh the father's evidence (the four facts above) in reaching a judgment.

E. USING CONTROLLING AUTHORITIES

After you provide the appellate court with context by your use of the important facts, connect how legal authorities apply. Rely upon the strongest available case law or statutes supporting your argument. Identify the strongest precedents and use them to make your argument.

Place these controlling precedents front and center in your argument. Then show how these major authorities are applied to the facts.

Do not list every relevant case on point.

Instead, focus on how the major supporting authorities are relevant and explain how they directly apply to your client's case.

What counts are not how many authorities you cite, but how well you articulate the controlling value contained within them. A single strong authority is all it may take to win the day.

Here is an example:

> This is not a novel case. This Court held, over twenty years ago, alimony must be *based upon the payor's ability to pay. Stanger v Stanger,* 47 Utopia 41 1997. This fundamental principle of alimony has not been altered by legislative action or court edict. It remains the law to this day. The Husband lacked the ability to pay alimony. He was unemployed at the time of divorce. Therefore, the Lower Court has made an error, which requires reversal.

F. NEGATIVE AUTHORITIES

What to do with negative authorities? Those pesky cases that are unsupportive of your argument?

Handle by aggressively contrasting negative authorities by distinguishing them from your case. Take the prior example from the opposing viewpoint.

> It is true this Court held, over twenty years ago, that alimony must be *based upon the payor's ability to pay. Stanger v Stanger,* 47 Utopia 41 1997. The Wife agrees with the brief of the Husband that the fundamental principle of alimony has not been altered by legislative action or court edict and remains the law to this day.

However, the Husband did not lack an ability to pay alimony. In contrast, he was not unemployed at the time of divorce, but rather supporting himself as an independent investor. His financial holdings providing him income, which afforded him the ability to pay alimony. *Kligman v Kligman*, 89 Utopia 107 (1993). Thus the Lower Court did not commit error and the judgment should be affirmed.

We know family law cases turn on *specific* facts. Make a factual case that contradictory authority does not apply to your case before the appellate court. Be candid. Do not ignore important authorities. Instead, confront and contrast by using facts.

G. USING PERSUASIVE AUTHORITIES

What if your appellate case lacks controlling authority?

Use the next best thing: persuasive authority. For example, argue other jurisdictions have adopted a similar rule on point to your matter.

PRACTICE POINTER

The weight of authority is determined by its reasoning in its ruling.

In addition, cite secondary authorities in your brief. Consider using law review articles, custodial studies, family law treatises, and case annotations to confirm the trend throughout the other states.

These secondary materials are important to use in family law. Perspectives grow and change over time on legal standards, particularly in the area of parenting-child custody.

There are numerous child development studies available to support your argument. Find one and use it if it is applicable.

PRACTICE POINTER

Be aware of emerging trends in the law when they are relevant to your case and use them to support your argument.

H. USE OF FOOTNOTES

One of the most difficult problems in appellate writing is deciding when to use footnotes.

Decisions by the highest appellate courts often contain hundreds of footnotes. It is found in the academic style.

But what should you do? Should you liberally use footnotes?

The answer is mostly no. Or, at a minimum, use footnotes with great caution.

You are not writing the appeals court opinion nor performing an academic exercise. There is no letter grade or gold star from the appellate court provided for your brief.

The readers of your brief are simply looking for arguments supported by proper citations and strong legal reasoning. Your function is to get your point across in a concise and persuasive manner. The excessive use of footnotes diminishes your very purpose.

One other footnote problem in brief writing.

The primary reason for avoiding extensive footnoting is it serves as a pause in the reader's mind. It causes the reader to look away and search for something.[67] Footnotes interrupt the flow of your argument and they distract your reader.[68] They cause your reader to fatigue. Your reader loses interest in your writing. And, well, there goes your argument.

There are, of course, some limited exceptions where footnotes might be both useful and necessary in your text. In certain situations, they are effective to keep your flow moving.

There might be times to set forth a number of examples to highlight the point you are making and where the use of multiple citations within your text would disturb the flow for your reader.

Consider the following example:

> All alimony awards granted by the lower court must be need based. *See Demoga v. Salerno,* 122 Utopia 199 (1995) (need based support shown by the recipient). *See Jacob v. Jenna,* 663 Utopia. 42 (1988) ("The common thread running through all alimony case law is that alimony is need based"), *appeal filed,*

---

67. See what I mean?

68. Again, do you see my point?

> No. 09-1709 (Utopia Supreme Judicial Court, November 22, 1988) (such as when a spouse is unable to maintain full time employment), *see, e.g., Katie v. Maggie,* 406 Utopia. 91 (1970); *New York v. New Jersey,* 2 Utopia 222 (1907); *Jenna v. Jacob* 12 Utopia 3 (2005).

Consider now the revised section, which includes exactly the same language, but with footnotes to enhance the presentation:

> All alimony awards granted by the lower court must be need based.[69] The spouse who is unable to work will need to demonstrate his or her incapacity.[70] A spouse can demonstrate incapacity in a number of ways.

Footnotes used sparingly enhance the comprehension of the information by allowing the text to be more readable. It prevents the distraction of multiple uses of citations in the text. It still allows your reader to "stop and check" your references but does not distract from the momentum of your presentation.

I. TECHNIQUES

One of the most effective techniques to utilize with authorities is to imbed quotations into arguments in your brief writing. It pays to quote directly from a case setting forth your major premise. This is particularly true when a statute or precedent might be dispositive of the issue in your appeal.

An example:

Our removal statute protects the noncustodial parent from the custodial parent removing a child without prior or parental permission from our state. The statute states in pertinent part:

> "A custodial parent cannot remove a child without prior permission by a Court of competent jurisdiction or the non-custodial parent. . . ."

---

69. Now the flow works by not interrupting the reader with excessive information.

70. By limiting your use of footnotes, your presentation is enhanced.

On October 31, 2017, the father, the custodial parent of the minor child, removed the minor child out of state without permission of the mother, the noncustodial parent of the minor child.

This example articulates the problem ahead for the reader. It is unnecessary to continue to quote the myriad of case law supporting the statute. When in doubt, always keep it simple. This brings us to the next point.

Use quotations sparingly. It does not help to string along quotation after quotation. From the Honorable Daniel M. Friedman (and yes—I understand the irony):

> "Quotations from cases are effective only if used sparingly. Quoting at length from opinion after opinion is a lazy way of writing a brief, and the finished product is likely to be unconvincing. Long before the brief approaches its end, the reader has begun to skip over quotations."[71]

Develop confidence in your presentation and your legal reasoning. You are not trying to win a "quotation battle." Appellate practice is not a game of legal Trivial Pursuit. State the law and support it by a direct citation. Move on to the next point.

Also avoid lengthy block quotations.

Why?

It invites your reader to skip over your lengthy and well-placed quotation that you were so thrilled to include in your brief. Appellate brief readers do not have the time to read lengthy quotes. It is similar to the excessive use of footnotes.

So what to do with quotations?

Find ways to make the precedents' words yours by incorporating them directly into your sentences. Here's a good example.

> In *Sara v. Joe*, 69 Utopia 186 (1962), this Court held lower courts cannot award trust property to a spouse of the other party when "the parties have been married less than ten years." *Sara*, 69 Utopia at 189.

71. ANTONIN SCALIA & BRYAN A. GARNER, MAKING YOUR CASE 128 (Thomson/West, 2008).

> As Justice Grant stated in *Green v. Angelo* "the most obvious limitation imposed by that requirement is parties need to have a mid-term or greater length of marriage to divide a beneficial of a party in a trust to the divorcing spouse." 54 Utopia at 78.

The use of imbedded quotes lends authenticity and force to your argument.

J. ERRORS TO AVOID

Fundamental writing skills are necessary for effective appellate practice. Writing errors are distracting. Grammatical errors are careless and diminish the strength of your argument.

It is impossible to catalogue all of the grammatical errors in appellate briefs, but some common errors are worth reviewing.

1. Run-on Sentences

Avoid the run-on sentence. This is a sentence that combines several clauses containing separate ideas into single expression. Make a singular point. Support that one point. Discuss how it applies to your facts. Conclude. Next point.

Do not attempt to link two points into one sentence. It will cause the run-on you are seeking to avoid.

Add complementary ideas in new sentences to support each singular point.

2. The Use of "That"[72]

Strive to not make the mistake of using the word *that* unnecessarily within your sentence. For example, *The judge then did that hearsay objection and that is an error of law.* Write instead, *The judge committed an error of law by sustaining the objection under hearsay grounds.*

This is a common mistake that[73] has crept into the English vernacular.

---

72. A confession. The author is very guilty of the overuse of the word *that*. Let's all strive to remove that!!

73. Yes, I am being facetious.

Pick up a newspaper and you find repetitive examples of this poor grammatical habit. The habit is even heard in everyday conversation.

Avoid *that* in your well-written brief.

3. Words Without Context

Be careful to use words set in proper context in your argument. Certain words may seem obvious to you, but if it is not entirely clear in your usage to your reader, it causes confusion. Avoid the use of unnecessary words.

For example, try this one: The husband received his degree while the wife only received her master's degree. The sentence begs the question as to what educational degree (or black belt in karate, perhaps?) the husband received. This uncertainty causes the reader to scratch his or head. In other words, flow is interrupted. Your job is to avoid any distractions to the reader.

Your presentation is improved by writing.

Both parties went to Harvard University for graduate school. The husband received his doctorate in psychology while the wife received her master's degree in business administration.

If you are positive the reader fully understands exactly what you are referring to, only then is your usage adequate. Otherwise, rewrite to remove any doubt.

4. The Use of "Only"

Another common mistake is the improper use or placement of the word *only*. Here is an example.

> Only from the most strained interpretation of the parties' separation agreement can the appellants argument means what appellants say.

Huh? The confusion is obvious.

5. Spelling

Always watch your spelling.

Most software programs correct numerous spelling errors, but there are times when repetitive words pass the spell check. For example, *there* and *their* both pass the software test, but one is incorrect in the usage.

The solution is to have your brief proofread to spot misspellings and typos missed by your smart computer. Reading your brief out loud will also help you catch errors.

6. Capitalization

Be consistent in your capitalization. If you use the word *court* with a lowercase *c*, then use it throughout your brief.

All of these bad habits, and many others, are corrected by devoting practice to improving your writing skills. Spend the time to improve your writing!

PRACTICE POINTER

Read books on the art of writing, and if you find one difficult to read, discard it immediately.

K. DRAFTING CONSIDERATIONS

Style is a critical component of a well-drafted appellate brief.

Your briefs are formal legal documents, but they do not serve the same purpose as other legal documents, such as legal contracts. A contract may include boilerplate terms because contracts have established legal meanings.

In a commercial relationship, the use of standard terms and meaning are important for the parties entering into the contract to understand the meaning of their written agreements.

But what about your appellate briefs?

An appellate brief is designed *to persuade* your reader.

A brief presents your client's position in the most favorable manner possible. But you must resist certain forms of style. For example, there is a temptation in family law to be overly emotional.

PRACTICE POINTER

Write your brief in a clear, direct, and consistent manner.

L. AVOID ANGER

> *"When you have no basis for an argument, abuse the plaintiff."*
>
> —Cicero

Do not express any anger in your brief. This is difficult in practice. After all, the purpose is to right an injustice for your client.

You want to strike back at the "moronic judge" who screwed your client. Right? You do. Do you feel the anger building up?

Ignore it.

Avoid the temptation to write angry prose. Check your emotions at the drafting table. You simply must avoid personal or disrespectful comments about trial judges or opposing counsel.

Here is an example.

You are appealing a custodial removal action where the judge did not apply the correct legal standard to your case. You review applicable case law and you stumble upon a case where your very same judge was overruled for applying the same incorrect standard in another case, where the appeals court overturned her decision. You are angry. You want to quote from the case and place within a footnote the following:

> Footnote 1 = Ironically, the lower court's judge was also the judge in *Green*, which was overturned by the appeals court. (Ha-ha.)
>
> Avoid this negative temptation to insult the trial judge in your brief.

M. BE STRAIGHTFORWARD

Ask for relief in a blunt, straightforward manner. When you effectively use clarity, your reader better understands your argument and is less inclined to question it. You are more persuasive.

In addition, clarity negates your opponent's attack upon your argument. There is no ambiguity in your argument to the court. You are understood and heard. Your client will be thankful.

PRACTICE POINTER

Use the facts without emotion and in a direct, matter-of-fact manner to tell your client's story.

N. USE YOUR OWN STYLE RATHER THAN EMOTION TO BE EFFECTIVE

How do you provide the persuasive pop to tell your client's story?

Say custody of a child is awarded by the trial judge to the wrong parent (other party) who moves out of state. How do you present *her* story? How do you present the human element? How can you make your story interesting and engaging?

Successful appellate practice is a combination of art and science.

The proper use of style allows you to present your arguments in a way to move the appellate judges.

You have a story to tell, so tell it by using style effectively.

O. DO NOT BE TOO ACADEMIC

Brief writing requires academic skills, but it is not an academic exercise.

It is an exercise in persuasion and requires different skills than those in the academic world. Yes, you need to apply research and understanding of case law and statutory interpretation. But your goal is persuasion by your use of reason.

Demonstrate why your argument is correct. Use your facts, the legal principles, new ideas, if necessary, and developing legal trends and build them to support your argument.

Never try to show off your intellectual ability.

P. AVOID FAMILY LAW JARGON

The appellate court may not be familiar with your use of your family law vernacular. As a result, avoid using family law jargon, or, at a minimum, ensure your readers understand exactly what you are meaning by a family law–related expression.

PRACTICE POINTER

Avoid being overly academic in your brief. Instead focus on the facts and your legal reasoning to make your argument.

Q. FURTHER CONSIDERATIONS

Almost all family law cases are decided in state courts.

The major exception is cases decided under the Hague Convention, which affords a litigant the right to pursue either state or federal action. Thus your matter is decided within your state's appellate court and/or the supreme court of your given state.

Most states have two levels of review: the intermediary level—your appeals court—and a final potential review within the highest court of your state. Some states have an appeals court of concurrent jurisdiction with the supreme court of the state. In those states, the supreme court sometimes has the right to "pluck" a matter from the appeals court.

For example, the Massachusetts Supreme Judicial Court has concurrent jurisdiction with the appeals court and can step in and remove a case from the appeals court. This is a common occurrence in important matters of family law.

It is important to maintain an understanding of the court to which you are drafting. When you draft a brief for an intermediate court of appeals, it is critical to understand such courts are controlled and advised by precedents set by higher courts, such as the state's supreme court or, certainly, even the U.S. Supreme Court.

It is important to note intermediate courts are influenced and interested in their own precedents, as well as the prior decisions of other intermediate courts in the jurisdiction.

Always consider the stature of the court for which you are arguing. The court's importance impacts the case precedents you are stating.

In intermediate courts of review, precedents from their superior courts have greater value. Point to authorities to support your argument when they are dispositive of your issues.

What about when they do not support your argument?

In the event precedents undermine your argument, never ignore them. It undermines your credibility with the appeals court. Instead, address those authorities and demonstrate how they do not apply. Or, how your matter differs from precedent and should produce a different result.

Consider in certain circumstances that arguing prior precedent should no longer control your issue. For example, perhaps a statute altered how alimony is configured and prior precedent no longer controls your matter.

Argue the rationale of the prior rule of law is no longer controlling due to the change in the statute.

And finally, if you can find no good faith basis for challenging existing law, then you conceded it in your brief.

Make a fact-based argument on hopefully rare occasions.

In other words, argue to the appeals court that the trial judge made a determinative error in the facts of your case. Argue that when you apply the *actual facts* to the law, it changes the result for your client. Certainly a higher bar, but sometimes your best option in a family law appeal.

R. DRAFTING TO YOUR STATE'S HIGHEST COURT

It requires a different approach when you are writing for your state supreme courts or even the U.S. Supreme Court.

Consider a supreme court has authority to change, limit, or overrule its own precedents. This is your opportunity to be a game changer.

This is not to state the highest courts readily alter existing law, and in fact, there is generally a reluctance to do so, but the opportunity to change and/or even shift existing law is available.

Point out how current law supports your argument and conversely, when appropriate for your client, how prior precedents should be altered.

If your matter is one of "first impression" or if there is a compelling reason it is likely to end up before your state's highest court, then design your brief with those considerations in mind.

In those instances, add public policy concerns to add a level of gravity to your brief. Anticipate the appellate court's concerns of how the legal issue involved affects future litigants when it is decided in favor of your client.

The idea of arguing before your highest court may sound either fun or terrifying to you, but it begs the question: How do you really know if you are going to appear before your jurisdiction's highest court?

Here are guidelines:

1. If you find a difference in legal precedents in other local appellate jurisdictions. When you are confronted with this scenario, raise the difference with the higher court for determination of the dispute.
2. If your case involves the interpretation of constitutional issues or questions first impression. When this occurs, point out to the court "this is a case of first impression."
3. Your matter involves the construction and/or validity of a newly enacted statute. Again, point out to the court the stature has not been reviewed by the supreme court.
4. Your court of appeals committed an error of law in its decision making, setting negative precedent on similarly situated litigants. When you face this type of issue, then argue to the higher court the decision is outrageous and requires correction. Of course, argue the point utilizing logic and reason in your persuasion, as you are now challenging not just a trial judge, but also the appellate court.
5. The inferior court of appeals issued a ruling on an important issue of law that should be weighed and decided by your jurisdiction's highest court.
6. Your case involves a unique or novel legal concept. This could be a case of first impression or something your legal instincts tell you should be considered by the highest court in your state. When you are confronted with such an issue, address it in your brief.

PRACTICE POINTER

If your case is of first impression or even novel, then write your brief, assuming it makes it to your state's supreme court.

S. AMICUS CURIAE

An amicus curiae is a third-party brief to assist the higher court in reaching a decision in a matter before the court. In reality, it is an advocacy brief for a certain proposition. The goal of the amicus brief is to broaden the higher court's understanding of an issue by providing a greater perspective on the issue and how a decision will affect other similar future litigants. In the event your case is of high importance, your state supreme court may solicit calls for amicus curiae to assist the court's decision making.

For example, your case has an alimony issue that, depending on the decision, could negatively affect recipients of support who stayed home and raised the children during the marriage.

You may wish to find a group advocating against changes in a state's alimony framework. A woman's advocacy group from your state bar association could be helpful to supplement the issue. The brief would focus on the viewpoint of nonworking mothers and the importance and critical need of alimony. It can include economic data and scientific evidence.

Keep in mind an amicus brief is not your own submission, but is rather an alignment of your position written by a third party with a similar goal.

These briefs are routinely written by special interest groups, individuals affected by a change of law but not parties, law professors, or sections of a state bar association. All are good candidates for you to suggest writing an amicus brief in your case.

T. FINAL PREPARATION BEFORE DRAFTING

When you are preparing to draft your brief, read sample briefs in the specific area of family law you are drafting. Find the seminal case for alimony, contribution to the marital estate, and/or child custody.

Read all briefs submitted (even the losing sides) and achieve an understanding of what came before you and what may be effective with your appellate court.

PRACTICE POINTER

After you draft the outline and before you begin drafting your brief, take time to read a well-written brief in the same topic area.

Briefs can be found now on individual appellate court websites. Use them as a resource. The more familiar you are with compelling briefs, the better your own brief will become. Now let's turn to formatting and avoiding the rejection of your brief.

11 How to Correctly Format, File Timely, and Avoid Rejection of Your Brief

A. AVOID REJECTION OF YOUR BRIEF

Appellate court rules require particular typefaces, font sizes, binding, color of the brief cover, and the method of service of the brief on opposing counsel. You need to be in compliance with all filing requirements to avoid rejection of your brief. There is no worse feeling than drafting a prodigious argument only to have it rejected due to improper binding and a wrongly utilized color.

Local rules establish the exact structural and format components required for your brief and any other required submissions.[74] An understanding of the following universal components will assist you in avoiding rejection of your brief.

PRACTICE POINTER

Check your state's appellate website for format requirements.

---

74. The Record Appendix, Certificate of Service, Statement of Compliance.

B. FORMATTING

Here are the general format requirements for briefs in almost every jurisdiction.[75]

1. Colors

The appellate brief is a blue cover and limited in length to no more than fifty pages.

The appellee's brief (the response brief but never the reply brief) is a red cover and limited in length to no more than fifty pages.

Any reply brief (not the response brief) is a gray cover and is limited in length to no more than twenty pages.

2. Binding

All briefs must be securely bound on the left-hand side. Some courts refuse circular binding. Avoid spiral binding and take the time to have your brief bound in compliance with your local rule.

3. Covers

All brief covers contain the name of the case; the appeals court docket number; the name of the trial court; the name of the lower court judge; the title of the document (i.e., Appellant's Brief); the filer's name, address, and telephone number; the e-mail addresses of any counsel representing the party on whose behalf the brief is filed; and, if an individual counsel is affiliated with a law firm, the firm name.

4. Margins

The margins must be 1.5 inches on the left and right, and 1 inch on the top and bottom.

The adoption of margin requirements was in response to "clever lawyers" who were utilizing smaller margins and or even smaller fonts or other clever devices to evade length requirements.

---

75. Another reminder to check your local rules. Be cognizant that the advent of electronic filing rules vary and change.

5. Types

The brief must be printed in black ink using a monospaced font, double spaced, on 8.5 by 11-inch white paper. Some jurisdictions require certain type and font size.

6. Fonts

So what is a monospaced font?

It is when each letter takes up the same amount of space as every other letter. The monospaced font most widely used and readily available on most word processing programs is Courier or Courier New, 12-point size. Use one of these. This is no knock on good ol' Times New Roman, of course. And keep in mind footnotes are required to be typed using the same font and point size.

Do not underestimate the importance of correct use of fonts. For example, in the state of Kansas they will reject your brief unless it is in 13-point Times New Roman, even if you file electronically!

C. WORD COUNT/PAGE LIMITS

The mission of your brief is not to write as many words as possible, but to persuade your reader of your correct argument. Never think you win any court points by stuffing excessive words into your brief. In fact, the opposite is more likely to result with the appeals court becoming annoyed as they read your overly verbose brief.

The page and/or word limits may depend upon the type of brief: appellant (if you are bringing the appeal), appellee (when you are responding to the appellant brief), and reply brief (when you are an appellant who is responding to the appellee brief).

Courts express a length limit and/or page limit or both. For example, the Federal Rules of Appellate Procedure limits a principal appellate brief to thirty pages or 14,000 words.

Many jurisdictions limit the length of the argument section. Or many jurisdictions require a summary of the argument, depending on the length of the argument section.

Check with your local court of appeals clerk's office, as you never want your brief rejected because of page limitations or formatting issues.

PRACTICE POINTER

Maintain your own checklist to prepare and draft your brief to ensure compliance with local rules.

D. NO GUIDELINES?

What if there are no formal guidelines?

Consult your local appellate court office. A telephone call to a helpful appellate clerk to check on requirements is never a bad idea when guidelines are unclear from a review of a court's website.

One other suggestion is review briefs previously submitted in other matters to confirm your format is in compliance.

Finally, use the table at the end of this book for appellate information pertaining to your local jurisdiction.

E. HARD COPIES OR E-FILING

As my daughter likes to say, "way back in the old days" all documents were filed by hardcopy in the courthouse and counsel attached a paper certificate of service.

Today, many courts are allowing and/or even requiring the electronic filing of all documents.

The appeals courts requiring electronic filings have very specific instructions. You must comply with any and all electronic requirements to the same level of completeness you apply to hand-delivering the documents..

It is good practice to confirm electronic submissions made it to the appeals court. You never want e-submissions to end up in the junk folder or in an unsent folder on your computer. The appeals court filing provides an electronic receipt, but it is best practice to check with the appeals court to ensure the brief and all materials filed are received. A quick telephone call to an appellate clerk to confirm receipt of electronic submissions of briefs is worth the time.

PRACTICE POINTER

Always file your brief twenty-four hours in advance of any deadline to confirm your brief was properly submitted and to allow time to correct any deficiencies.

F. NUMBER OF COPIES

What if you are hard filing your brief?

The U.S. Supreme Court requires forty copies of your brief in most circumstances. Here is one state court example.

The state of Oklahoma requires that "one original and fourteen copies of the brief shall be filed for every brief."[76]

This is a typical example of the approximate number of briefs that states require. Local practice dictates the precise number of copies. As always, be in compliance with your local rules.

G. SIGNATURE REQUIRED AND DO NOT FORGET TO DATE

Most appeals courts require your signature at the end of your brief. Be sure to date your signature as well.

Presume a handwritten signature is required in a hard copy of any brief submitted to the court. End with:

Respectfully submitted,

____

Your signature.

Date

H. ELECTRONIC SIGNATURE

What if you are electronically filing your brief?

---

76. Oklahoma Supreme Court Rule 1:10.

The general rule adopted for electronically filed documents is an electronically generated signature or "s/typed name." For example, the federal third circuit's local appellate rule 46.4 provides "all documents, motions, and briefs must be signed by an attorney or by a party appearing *pro se*. Electronically filed documents must be signed with an electronically generated signature or 's/typed name.'"

This e-method of signature is likely to change over time as more sophisticated methods of technology are adopted, but is currently accepted in the federal jurisdictions.

But end your brief in the same manner as a handwritten copy with "respectfully submitted" followed by "s/typed name."

I. CERTIFICATE OF SERVICE

Most appeals courts require certification of service upon opposing counsel.

In New York State, for example, the rule states "the original affidavit of service shall be affixed to the inside of the back cover of the original of each paper filed."[77]

The major difference found within local rules is some jurisdictions may require service at the time the brief is filed with the appeals court while other courts may allow service after the brief is filed.

In either event, a certificate of service is generally required, and more importantly, it is better practice to always file one.

If your jurisdiction allows for an electronic filing of your brief, you may be able to serve your brief electronically to the other side.

In most courts, where electronic filings are allowed, the court requires you to register for these services and only counsel or parties who completed the local requirements are allowed to use the e-filing system.

Review your local rules, and if necessary encourage your opposing counsel to register electronically to ensure electronic submissions are allowed for all parties.

77. Court of Appeals State of New York, Part 500 Rules of Practice.

PRACTICE POINTER

Always register with your appeals court if electronic filings are permitted to save time and money for the production of briefs. It is also the trend across the country in appellate practice. Do not be left behind.

The universal components of a certificate of service are how and when you provide the filings to your party opponent.

Here is a sample:

CERTIFICATE OF SERVICE

I certify I have hand delivered one copy of the foregoing brief to Counsel of the Appellee, A Petruccelli at her address, 100 Santarpio Street, Utopia, on March 1, 2018.

's; George Washington

George Washington

100 Virginia Street

Washington, DC 01100

Counsel for the Appellant

J. CERTIFICATION OF COMPLIANCE

States require certification to the appellate court be in compliance with all appellate court rules. This certification is different from "the certificate of service."

The purpose of this rule, which is a fairly new requirement of appellant practice, is to ensure compliance with the court's format, including word or page count. It is your promise to the court of compliance with all court rules.

Here is a sample certification from Minnesota:[78]

I hereby certify this document conforms to the requirements of the applicable rules, is produced with a [monospaced]

78. Minnesota Rules of Appellate Practice Rule 16(k).

> [proportional] font, and the length of this document is [lines] [words]. This document was prepared using [name and version of word processing software].
>
> _________________________
>
> SIGNATURE

States require the last page of every brief to contain a statement that certifies you complied with the filing and rules required for your brief.

K. TIME STANDARDS FOR SUBMISSION OF BRIEFS

All states issue time standards for the submissions of briefs. The appellant is generally allowed forty to forty-five days from the date the appeals court places the matter on the docket.

For example, the state of Wisconsin rule states, "The brief of appellant must be filed no later than '40' days after the filing of the record on appeal with the clerk of the court of appeals."[79]

States afford slightly less time to file an appellee brief. Most rules provide thirty days to file your appellee brief after service of the brief by the appellant.[80]

Many states issue a "scheduling order" stating the time deadlines for briefs and all materials to be submitted to the appeals court.

In West Virginia, the rule is a scheduling order issues:[81] "As soon as practicable after the proper filing of the notice of appeal. . ."

And it will contain:

> As appropriate to the circumstances, the scheduling order will contain the dates on which the petitioner's brief, the response brief, the reply brief, and the designated record or appendix shall be filed; will set forth whether a transcript will be prepared, the extent of any transcript, and the date the transcript is due; will set forth deadlines for filing motions; and may set forth such other matters as deemed beneficial or necessary. The

79. Wisconsin Rules of Appellate Procedure Rule 809.19.
80. *Id.*
81. West Virginia Judiciary, Rules of Appellate Procedure Rule 10.

scheduling order will set forth the official caption of the case on appeal that should be used on the cover page of all documents filed with the Court.

L. EXPEDITED APPEALS

State rules permit certain expedited appeals, and many of these touch upon family law matters. For example, states allow juvenile matters to be heard on an expedited basis or matters involving the termination of parental rights. States may allow for an expedited appeal when it involves child custody.

For example, in North Carolina, the rule allows for an expedited brief when a party is appealing a case involving termination of parental rights and issues of juvenile dependency or juvenile abuse and/or neglect.[82]

Always consider when "timeliness" is critical to expedite an appeal, particularly if there are local rules allowing it.

A removal judgment permitting relocation of a child out of state is an excellent example. If a rule does not allow for an expedited appeal, then consider seeking such relief by way of motion to the court along with the applicable motion to stay the order.

Practice Pointer

In matters of interstate custody, an expedited appeal must always be seriously considered.

M. TIME FOR EXTENSION OF TIME

But, hey, what if there is not enough time to complete your brief? Don't panic. Most, if not all, states afford an extension of time to file your brief.

In Massachusetts, for example, a request for additional time to file a brief is brought by filing a "Motion for Enlargement of

82. North Carolina Rules of Appellate Procedure Rule 3A.

Time."[83] The rule allows "the appellate court or a single justice for good cause shown may upon motion enlarge the time prescribed by these rules or by its order for doing any act, or may permit an act to be done after the expiration of such time . . ."

PRACTICE POINTER

Do not wait until the last minute to file a motion for enlargement of time. It saves time to plan ahead and determine when you can realistically submit your brief.

The reality is most appellate lawyers seek an extension of time.

Like any good motion, articulate your reasoning for why you require additional time to complete your brief. Add a detailed affidavit to support your motion.

The California rule articulates appropriate grounds for an extension, such as adequate time for preparation of accurate and complete submissions to assist the courts; other deadlines as a practical matter preclude filing the document by the due date without impairing its quality, illness, a personal emergency, or a planned vacation.[84]

PRACTICE POINTER

You are likely to be granted an extension of time to file your brief, but take the motion seriously and provide sufficient detail to ensure the court grants your motion to extend time for filing of your brief.

N. REJECTION

All appellate courts take formatting and timely filing of briefs seriously. Appellate courts clerks reject briefs for failure to follow formatting requirements, submitting the incorrect number of briefs, and missing time standards.

83. Massachusetts Rule of Appellate Procedure Rule 14.
84. California Rules of Court Rule 45.5.

Here is one local rule with applicable appellate court commentary to consider:

> The justices take the formatting of briefs very seriously and the clerk's office will reject briefs for failure to follow formatting requirements and other requirements as specified in the Rules of Appellate Procedure.
>
> If the court determines a brief does not comply with the rules, the filer will be told what needs to be corrected and will be given time to make those corrections. A Motion to File Nonconforming Brief may be filed if compliance with the rules is not possible.[85]

O. BUT WHAT IF I AM . . .

If the appellate court determines a brief does not comply with the prescribed rules, you are informed what requires correction and given a period of time to correct your submissions. This causes you and your client anxiety, time, and money. Moreover, if you attempt to circumvent the rules, you may run into some serious trouble with your appeals court.

Cheating on font size, margins, and spacing in order to comply with the page limits "tells the judges that the lawyer is the type of sleaze ball who is willing to cheat on a small procedural rule and therefore probably will lie about the record or forget to cite controlling authority."[86]

Just ask one New York City law firm that incurred the wrath of a federal judge by not following format rules.

The law firm, Susman Godfrey, was fined $1,048.09 for improper "spacing" submitted in a brief.[87] The firm was attempting to cram more words into its argument on behalf of Amazon.

---

85. Massachusetts Rules of Appellate Procedure Rule 1, 16, 19, 20.

86. Rambo and Pflaum, Legal Writing by Design § 20.3, p. 344 (2001) (quoting Judge Alex Kozinski, *The Wrong Stuff*, B.Y.U.L. Rev. 325 at 327, 1992).

87. Debra Cassens Weiss, *ABA Journal: Susman Godfrey Is Sanctioned for Wrong Line Spacing in Brief*, ABA Journal, April 4, 2017.

U.S. District Judge Victor Marrero found the law firm used 24-point spacing, rather than double spacing, allowing it to exceed the court's twenty-five-page limit. According to Marrero, the court's individual rules of practice require all memoranda to be "double-spaced and in 12-point font with 1-inch margins."

Marrero declared "the flouting of this court's individual rules" was a deliberate choice by the law firm "to gain some slight advantage in this litigation."

There are other examples.

A federal judge in Louisiana took lawyers to task in 2014 for slightly squeezing the spacing between the lines.

In the "old days" of typewriters, single-spaced type had 12 points per line and double spaced had 24 points per line. But "double spaced" in many word processing programs adds even more breathing room, which reduces the number of lines per page.

The lesson here is to take the time to be in full compliance with your local formatting rules and avoid any attempt to be "smart" and "cute" with these rules.

Get it right the first time. It is time well spent to comply with the local rules and submit proper brief and supporting materials.

In summary, consider the format and timeliness of your brief as equally important to your argument to persuade your reader. Take the appellate court's rules and regulations seriously. Ensure full compliance with your local rules when you submit any brief; file an extension of time if needed; and ensure your brief is accepted and not rejected by your appellate court.

The Universal Elements of a Brief and Writing with Persuasive Style

12

The structural aspects of a brief are found within local procedural rules. But there are some structural elements and requirements always present in each jurisdiction.

A. ELEMENTS OF THE BRIEF AND WHY IT IS IMPORTANT

First, it is critical that your brief and submissions present as a cohesive product to your reader. Never assume each appellate judge reads all of your submissions. Initially, for example, judges may only scan your submissions to gain an initial understanding of the major issues presented.

Thereafter, your brief and supporting materials may be more critically reviewed to determine if there is an error of law or an abuse of discretion and whether it is a potential error requiring appellate court action.

Or conversely, existing case law is sufficient to sustain the judgment of the lower court.

This initial review by your reader is why your presentation is critical. Your presentation guides and ultimately influences your reader. It leads to the direction your brief may take in the appellate court.

The first element of your brief is the table of contents. It is an outline of your argument. Issues are phrased in a manner to attract your reader's attention.

The second element is the statement of facts, which articulates your client's story and sets the stage to support your client's argument. The next element is your argument.

Your argument explains your legal reasoning. It directly connects to the factual context you provide in the statement of facts.

Your argument contains a conclusion wrapping up the justification of the relief you are seeking, or why your opponent's relief should be denied.

The order of your arguments can determine the brief's overall persuasiveness. A strongly and properly presented argument powerfully impacts your readers.

B. UNIVERSAL ELEMENTS OF YOUR BRIEF

The major requirements of a brief are universally subject to some local minor variations. For example, Massachusetts requires the following for all briefs:[88]

> (1) . . . a table of contents, with page references, and a table of cases (alphabetically arranged), statutes and other authorities cited, with references to the pages of the brief where they are cited.
>
> (2) A statement of the issues presented for review.
>
> (3) A statement of the case, which shall first indicate briefly the nature of the case, the course of proceedings, and its disposition in the court below. There shall follow a statement of the facts relevant to the issues presented for review, with appropriate references to the record (see subdivision (e)).
>
> (4) The argument, which shall contain the contentions of the appellant with respect to the issues presented, and the reasons therefor, with citations to the authorities, statutes, and parts

88. Massachusetts Rules of Appellate Practice Rule 16.

> of the record relied on. In a brief with more than twenty-four pages of argument, there shall be a short summary of argument, suitably paragraphed and with page references to later material in the brief dealing with the same subject matter, which should be a condensation of the argument actually made in the body of the brief, and not a mere repetition of the headings under which the argument is arranged. The appellate court need not pass upon questions or issues not argued in the brief. Nothing argued in the brief shall be deemed to be waived by a failure to argue orally.
>
> (5) A short conclusion stating the precise relief sought.
>
> (6) Any written or oral findings or memorandum of decision by the court pertinent to an issue on appeal included as an addendum to the brief.
>
> (7) In cases where geographical facts are of importance, unless appropriate plans are reproduced in the printed record or Record Appendix, an outline plan or chalk (preferably based on exhibits in evidence) shall be included. This outline plan should be suitable for reproduction on one page of the printed law reports.

States may have certain requirements in family law matter. For example, Alaska requires for divorce appeals:[89]

> (K) If the appeal concerns a property division in a divorce case, an appendix consisting of a table listing all assets and liabilities of the parties as reflected in the record, including the trial court's findings as to the nature (marital or individual), value, and disposition of each asset or liability.

Let's examine more closely the nearly universal brief requirements.

C. THE TABLE OF CONTENTS

A table of contents serves first as a reference for the appellate court. Use it for more than just a guide of what is ahead for your readers. Instead make it read as a summary of your argument. Attract your reader to the argument contained within your brief.

89. Alaska Rules of Appellate Procedure Rule 212(c)(1)[k].

If you followed my directive to prepare a detailed outline, a proper table of contents is easy to prepare and follows easily from your outlining.

The specific components of your table of contents are found within your local rule. The components are:

1. The table of contents.
2. The index of authorities.
3. The statement of the issues upon which the appeal is based.
4. The statement of facts, with subheadings summarizing important segments of the story.
5. The summary of the argument.
6. The argument with a separate statement of the issue and the argument under each issue, with subheadings summarizing important segments of the argument.
7. A conclusion and prayer for relief.
8. A certificate of service.
9. Addendum (if needed).

D. THE INDEX OF AUTHORITIES

The next required component is your index of authorities. This is your opportunity to assist your reader in the location of materials relied upon to support your argument.

Do not overlook its importance because you want to make it simple and easy for your reader to find supporting information at any time he or she is searching for it.

E. CITATION FORM

Use proper form in citing authorities both in your index and in your brief. Be familiar with the proper required citations of your local jurisdiction. Use the required format in all submissions and be consistent with your citation use. Inconsistent citation makes a bad impression upon your reader.

PRACTICE POINTER

Have a good proofreader for every brief you write to check not only format but also your citations.

F. THE STATEMENT OF THE ISSUE (OR ISSUES)

This is what any brief is really all about. There is no more important section than your framing of your issues for your argument. It is your purpose as to why you are before the appellate court. The heart and soul of your brief.

Use it as a succinct opportunity to demonstrate why your client deserves relief.

By definition, the statement of issues is what it sounds like, where your issues are "stated"—to the court.

You inform the appeals court what your brief is about. As the appellant, you point out the errors the lower court made and why the judgment requires reversal.

In contrast, when you represent the appellee, tell the court why there are no errors in the judgment and why the judgment should be affirmed.

You can utilize many different styles in framing issues in your argument. Here are some examples to consider:

1. You can simply pose a direct question, such as "Did the trial court make an error by awarding alimony to the wife?"
2. You can phrase the issue more indirectly: "Whether the lower court abused its discretion by awarding alimony."
3. Or you can be very direct: "Whether the lower court abused its discretion by awarding alimony above the husband's ability to pay the wife." In this example, you are beginning to lay the groundwork of your argument.

Consider stating why the error was prejudicial, such as: "The trial court erred in failing to consider the wife's income in fashioning the alimony award from the husband to the wife."

Another common method of phrasing is when you include the standard of review within your framing of your issue.

For example, "Did the trial court abuse its discretion in not considering the wife's part-time income?"

Create concise and direct statements to demonstrate issues to be presented. In doing so, add your own slant to direct the appeals court where you are going with your argument.

Finally, rely on fewer issues rather than more to not overwhelm the appellate court.

It is better to highlight *just* the important legal mistakes and not attempt to raise every single possibility. Brevity is the better rule.

PRACTICE POINTER

Less is more in determining the statement of your issues on appeal.

G. STATEMENT OF FACTS

There is no question that facts are demonstrative in all family law matters. The statement of facts is integral in building your argument. The facts precede the legal argument section of your brief.

The facts, not the law, are the human element of your appellate argument. It is your best opportunity to engage your reader with your storytelling.

Use your facts to tell your reader a compelling story. The entire legal argument must be tied closely to the "story" of the case you are telling your reader. Cite often to the record in your use of facts.

PRACTICE POINTER

You should be a great storyteller, and arranging how you tell the tale is a critical component to writing an excellent brief.

Your brief provides an understanding as to why the alleged error made by the trial judge requires a reversal. Demonstrate the injustice to have it corrected. The judicial sense of "equity" matters, particularly in a family law appeal. After all, family law matters are all about equitable fairness.

Never consider your statement of facts as only a summary of your version of events in the trial court. Rather, formulate your story and emphasize the critical events to support your arguments.

Be both accurate and persuasive in your statement of the facts.

Your mission is not only to be compelling but also to be informative. You are free to relocate critical facts into where you believe they provide the greatest impact upon your reader.

Connect those facts to the legal argument to come next.

As Judge Posner has written:

> *An effective advocate should point out "what if anything turns on the outcome of the case either for the parties or for some larger community."*[90]

Use the facts to introduce the story.

In addition, never use facts not contained in the record. Always include proper citations to the record to support the facts you are utilizing.

H. WHAT DO YOU DO WITH "BAD FACTS"?

Never ignore the "bad facts" in your statement of the facts.

Instead place negative facts into your own perspective. Use your argument to explain and/or contrast the bad facts with other crucial events. Demonstrate how the conclusion in your argument is proper and sound inclusive of any negative events.

For example, in a divorce action with a custodial battle, explain how the husband's conduct in having an affair did not prevent him from being the primary custodial parent of the parties' children during the marriage.

90. Eva M. Guzman, quoting Judge Posner from *Practical Considerations: Seeking Review in Courts of Last Resort*, 34 ABA Family Law Advocate, no. 4, 2014.

PRACTICE POINTER

Be prepared to confront negative facts at all stages of the appellate process.

I. USE FLOW IN YOUR WRITING

It is important to address the use of flow in your writing again. It is critical in your "statement of facts" flows to write seamlessly to capture your reader's attention.

Be direct. Be concise.

Effectively use headings and subheadings to guide the reader.

Headings are designed as small summaries, such as "The Husband's Income History" or "The Wife's Role as Primary Caregiver of the Children."

Use these signposts to assist the reader and provide momentum to the story you are telling.

PRACTICE POINTER

When writing the statement of facts, ensure that by the time your reader finishes, they want to know what happens next when you apply the law to your argument.

J. THE USE OF CITATIONS

Statement of facts are supported by citations to the record. Keep in mind your brief is reviewed for accuracy. As a result, support the "facts" with appropriate citations to your Record Appendix.

K. THE USE OF INFERENCES

Draw inferences from the facts in the record. But avoid imputing knowledge to a party when there is no evidence found within the record. Connect inferences to an event in the record to draw a logical conclusion. Cite the event to your Record Appendix.

For example, the husband's bank account at the time of divorce is $100,000 less than at the time of the divorce filing. You logically deduce he spent the $100,000 after the divorce filing. Thereafter, argue the effect of his postdivorce spending.

One caveat on your use of inferences in your brief.

An overreliance on inferences leads the reader to conclude your argument is unsubstantiated. An unsubstantiated argument is dead on arrival in the appellate court. A well-cited statement of facts supports your argument and avoids your brief tangling without support.

In summary, statements of facts are used to persuade and exemplify your argument. In fact, like everything else in your brief, *it must make your argument.*

L. THE SUMMARY OF THE ARGUMENT

Appeals courts sometimes require a summary of your argument. The longer the brief, the more likely you are required to include a summary of your argument.[91]

Regardless of the rule, always include a summary of your argument.

Why?

Because the summary of your argument might be the only item the appellate judge reads. From one authority:

> The summary may be . . . the only part of the brief some judges will ever read, either because they find the case simple enough to decide without further study or because they are overloaded with work, or simply unwilling to work very hard.[92]

Likewise, the summary of the argument might be the first thing read by the appeals court staff. Always make a good and strong first impression.

Unlike an introduction, the summary of argument is not just your preview of the topics contained within your argument. Rather, it is a condensed version of the substance of your argument.

---

91. See Massachusetts Rules of Appellate Procedure Rule 16.

92. Scalia & Garner, Making Your Case 97, quoting Robert L. Stern (Thomson/West, 2008).

How long or short should your summary of your argument be? After all, it is still a summary.

In their book *Making Your Case*, the late Justice Scalia and Bryan A. Garner suggest the following: "In a 50-page brief, we recommend no more than five pages and ideally no more than three."[93]

A good rule of thumb is three to five pages for your family law briefs.

M. THE GOAL OF THE SUMMARY OF YOUR ARGUMENT

The "summary of argument" section serves as an opportunity to present an overview of your complete argument to follow and attract the appellate court's attention to your major points.

Use it to showcase the unifying themes of your argument and as an opportunity to explain how your arguments are related.

For example, if one argument supports reversing the wrongfully decided marital division of assets while another supports remanding for a new trial on the issue of child support, then this is the place to make the distinction. By doing so, the court knows exactly the relief you are seeking.

State the main points of your argument clearly. To avoid any distraction to your reader, cite only key cases when necessary. Major points are understandable. The substantive details, such as case citations and statutory precedents, follow in your forthcoming argument.

PRACTICE POINTER

Write the summary of your argument only after you have written your argument.

N. THE ARGUMENT

Consider the argument section the "brain" of your brief. It is your logic.

Two critical points: First, keep your eye on what is important. Recall your outline, theme, and salient points to win the day. Forget the rest and eliminate any fluff.

93. *Id.*

Include nothing irrelevant to the argument you are presenting. Never get lost within your drafting and lose sight of the major points to be made.

And second, strive to be "brief." This is not a joke.

Help your client understand the importance of brevity and how it takes time to compose.

> *"I have made this longer than usual because I have not had time to make it shorter."*
>
> —Pascal

If your brief is overly verbose, it deflates your argument. You bore your reader, and your brief is sent to the affirmed pile when you are representing the appellant.

Brevity requires laser focus on removing everything not advancing your major arguments. It requires discipline. But in the end your use of brevity improves your persuasion.

Eliminate those weak points in your arguments that only add length to your brief. Any point not supporting your major argument is discarded.

When you are uncertain about removing points from your argument, ask the following question: Does this point move the ball? What would happen if I eliminate it?

If the answer is the argument can stand without the particular point, then remove it.

Practice Pointer

Always be eloquently brief in your argument.

O. THE CONCLUSION AND PRAYER FOR RELIEF

There are a few different approaches to close your brief. You can conclude with a simple prayer for relief. This is a perfectly acceptable approach, particularly if what has come before concisely makes your argument, and in many states all that is required by rule.

In fact, the office of the solicitor general of the United States takes this approach with a simple closing of only: "The judgment should be affirmed."[94]

Certainly, there are times it makes sense to simply ask the court what you are seeking in conclusion and state nothing further.

For example, when you are representing the appellee and you have written a short response to an inarticulate brief, which stands little chance of obtaining relief.

On those occasions, the court may have had enough and you may want to use a simple and short prayer asking to affirm the lower court's judgment.

But more often you choose to be more ambitious.

The request for relief is actually an integral part of your family law appeal. It is the last opportunity to signal to the court what you are asking them to do. Use it.

The request can be seeking a reversal or a remand with critical instructions.

For example, what happens with the alimony judgment now satisfied, but you are still asking the court to reverse it?

Given that the amount of alimony owed under the judgment is now satisfied by your client, you need to fashion your prayer accordingly. You want the appellate court to not deem the matter "moot" or less important.

In this example, try the following: "The matter should be returned to the lower court to not only vacate the alimony judgment, but also to determine a credit to be applied against the marital division of property in light of the reversal of the alimony judgment."

PRACTICE POINTER

Leave no doubt as to what you are seeking from the appellate court.

There are two more reasons to support writing a more detailed conclusion.

94. SCALIA & GARNER, MAKING YOUR CASE 100.

First, a summation is an additional opportunity to persuade your reader. And second, never pass on one final opportunity to demonstrate the impact of your argument.

A more powerful conclusion is accomplished by the following methods:

1. Focus on writing a powerful summary of your argument demonstrating your main points.
2. Alternatively, consider one or even two paragraphs stating your logic but in a new and creative manner.

For example, imagine a scenario in which the husband sought to terminate his alimony obligation to the wife, and the trial court found no material change in circumstances to warrant a termination of his alimony obligation.

Here is an example of a conclusion combining both of the approaches:

> In conclusion, it is clear the judgment issued by the Lower Court was not an abuse of discretion based upon recent precedent issued by the Supreme Judicial Court and subsequent Appeals Court decisions interpreting "the Act."
>
> The parties' "pre-Act" separation agreement contains an agreed upon termination date, which can only be modified by a showing by the Husband of a material change in his circumstances.
>
> The Lower Court, without the benefit of these rulings, issued a complete and thorough examination of each individual argument the Husband could make to terminate alimony in its Memorandum of Decision under the "Act" and found there has been no significant change to warrant termination of the Husband's alimony obligation. This is not an abuse of judicial discretion. Thus the Lower Court's judgment and reasoning should be affirmed.

The decision to employ which method—a short request for relief or a more detailed closing—depends upon your own writing style. A consideration is whether you are representing the appellant or the appellee. Space may play a critical role in your ability to add a longer closing. Choose your last words wisely for each brief.

P. REQUEST FOR ATTORNEY FEES

Family law appeals afford an opportunity to obtain attorneys' fees from your party opponent. An award of fees is usually highly discretionary and not every matter warrants a request for your fees. Take the following example:

A father does not want to pay child support consistent with his income to his ex-girlfriend, the child's mother. The law is clear and the judgment is well supported by the evidence. But the father persists in challenging say, the "constitutionality" of the court's power to order child support.

The mother now has to respond to the father's frivolous appeal. She should request appellate fees from the appeals court.

This is particularly true when it is virtually certain the judgment will be upheld: "if a judgment is affirmed or reversed in part, or is vacated, costs shall be allowed only as ordered by the appellate court."[95]

The Michigan rule is "the trial court may rule on requests for costs or attorney fees under MCR 2.403, 2.405, 2.625 or other law or court rule, unless the Court of Appeals orders otherwise."[96]

Attorney fees and costs are requested by motion or as a prayer for relief at the conclusion of the brief.

In Massachusetts, the following simple request is required. "The appellee/mother respectfully demands her appellate attorney's fees and costs be paid by the appellant/father in accordance with *Fabre v. Walton*, 441 Mass. 1030 (2004)."

Keep in mind in some jurisdictions, such as Texas, you may need to ask for appellate attorney's fees at trial.[97] A prevailing party must present evidence of appellate attorney's fees at trial in order to be entitled to claim them. A failure to present such evidence waives the claim for attorneys' fees.

In contrast, a nonprevailing party does not waive her claim for attorney's fees by failing to present such evidence. When the issue

95. Massachusetts Rules of Appellate Procedure Rule 26.

96. Michigan Appellate Rule 7.

97. Troy Hornsby, *Appellate Attorney's Fee Awards*, http://millerjames.com/2013/10/09/%EF%BF%BCappellate-attorneysfee-awards.

of appellate attorney's fees is properly preserved at trial, it can be addressed by the appellate court.

PRACTICE POINTER

Ask for attorney fees and costs any time you are responding to a less-than-meritorious brief.

Q. SPECIAL RULES OF CONTENT

Family law appeals can require additional content in briefs, depending on local rules. For example, the parties and the children's names may be required to be changed or only initials used.

Check your local rules carefully, particularly if your matter involves children. Often, when an appeal involves a child, special rules do attach for material inclusion in your brief.

For example, the state of Oregon requires the following:[98]

> In a dissolution proceeding or a proceeding involving modification of a dissolution judgment, *the summary of facts shall begin with the date of the marriage, the ages of the parties, the ages of any minor children of the parties, the custody status of any minor children, the amount and terms of any spousal or child support ordered, and the party required to pay support.*

In West Virginia, the following rules apply to matters involving children.[99]

1. **Responsibilities of guardian ad litem.** The guardian ad litem for any minor child involved in an abuse and neglect appeal must file a brief—or a summary response in an appropriate case—and if argument is held, the guardian must appear and present argument unless otherwise specifically ordered by the court.

98. Oregon Rules of Appellate Procedure, Rule 5.40(10).
99. West Virginia Rules of Appellate Procedure, Rule 11(h)–(j).

2. **Special requirements for briefs.** In addition to the items required by Rule 10, the briefs filed by the parties (including the guardian ad litem) *must contain a section immediately following the concise summary of argument required by Rule 10(c)(5), setting forth the current status of the minor children and any plans for permanent placement, and the current status of the parental rights of all the children's parents.*
3. **Update regarding the current status of the child.** *The parties shall provide a written statement of any change in the circumstances that were set forth in the briefs within one week of any oral argument scheduled by the court or within such other time as may be specified by order.*

R. ADDENDUM

A few states require an "addendum" of materials in your brief. The general requirements are to provide the applicable statutes, cases from out of state, or jurisdiction and/or cases "unpublished" within your jurisdiction.

When you are required to submit an addendum, you are tempted to just reprint a statute from Lexis, Bloomberg, or Westlaw. However, it is far better to reprint the applicable material in a Word version and use required type and margins required by your local rule.

Why? You always want to make material clear and easy to read for the appellate court.

PRACTICE POINTER

Always present any document to the appeals court in the most reader-friendly manner in compliance with your local rules.

In summary, consult local rules to meet all required elements of your brief. Use your preparation, an outline, and Record Appendix to make the brief's creation consistent with your theme and your argument. Keep a sharp eye on presentation and the required structure. Use the required elements to your advantage to produce a logical and sound argument that directly ties to the record in your case.

Now let's turn to some specific considerations for when you represent the appellee.

13 Some "Brief" Considerations When You Represent the Appellee

There are similar, if not the same, rules when you are representing the appellee, but there are vastly different considerations. Your function is still to persuade, but your role is to be supportive of the judgment rather than pointing out deficiencies.

A. CAPTIONS

The party submitting the first brief of an appeal or the opening brief is called the *appellant*. The party responding to the brief is the *appellee*, or sometimes the *respondent*.

You are not drafting a "reply" brief when you are the appellee or respondent. This improper caption is a common error to avoid at all costs.

There are times when you draft a cross appeal when you may potentially be either the appellant or the appellee. Usually, the designation hinges on who filed first—appellant—and who filed thereafter—appellee.

If there is an issue with designation of the parties, attempt to resolve it with opposing counsel. Only as a last resort should you file a motion with the appellate court to solve the problem.

B. FORMAT

Format and requirements for the appellee slightly differ from those of the appellant. For example, the state of Wisconsin requires the following format for an appellee or respondent:[100]

> **Brief of Respondent:** The Brief of Respondent is due to be filed thirty (30) days after the service of the Brief of Appellant (plus "3" days from the date of mailing if the Brief of Appellant is served by mail).

Note the appellee is titled the respondent. There is a shorter interval to file your brief than the time allowed when you are the appellant. This is true under most local rules.

The appellee brief is a response to the brief filed by the party who is appealing. When you represent the appellee, you are explaining why the trial court reached the correct judgment. Your role is to support the judgment rather than challenge it.

C. THE APPELLEE STATEMENT OF THE ISSUES AND THE CASE

An appellee may omit the statement of issues and the statement of the case if you are in agreement with the appellant.

Regardless of the right to omit the statement of the case, take the opportunity to frame your case in the most favorable light for your client by writing your own statement.

Be mindful of the words of former Justice Scalia: "Take every available occasion to shape how the judge views your case."[101]

---

100. Wisconsin Rules of Appellate Procedure Rule 809.19.

101. SCALIA & GARNER, MAKING YOUR CASE 60.

Here is another appellee rule example from the state of Georgia:[102]

b) Appellee.

The brief of appellee shall be divided in the following manner:

1. Part One shall point out any material inaccuracy or incompleteness of appellant's statement of facts and any additional statement of facts deemed necessary, plus citations to additional parts of the record or transcript deemed material.

The rule provides further direction for what the court is expecting in your brief. This rule is similar to how many states allow you to skip the statement of facts section in your appellee brief.

The rule continues:

> Failure to do so shall constitute consent to a decision based on the appellant's statement of facts. Except as controverted, appellant's statement of facts may be accepted by this Court as true.[103]

Use the general rule of persuasion to never miss an opportunity to frame a matter in your client's viewpoint.

The only time to skip an unrequired statement of the case or statement of facts is if there is absolutely no factual dispute between the parties.

In this scenario, you are demonstrating only the wisdom of the legal analysis of the lower court. Then the rule of brevity in brief writing is likely wise to apply.

PRACTICE POINTER

When you represent the appellee, take every opportunity to support the trial court's judgment.

Let's continue to examine the Georgia rule for special content requirements.

---

102. Georgia Court of Appeals Rules, Rule 23(b)(1).
103. *Id.*

2. Part Two shall contain appellee's argument and the citation of authorities as to each enumeration of error. It shall also include the standard of review if different from that contended by the appellant.[104]

Note here the requirement to denote case law supporting your arguments and the applicable standard of review. This section provides a choice of agreeing with the appellant and accepting the appellant's authorities and/or standard of review.

Again, do not simply agree with the appellant.

Continue to be active in your appellee response. Use contrast with the appellant's brief to effectively argue your own points supporting the judgment. Here is a simple example to illustrate the point of effectively using contrast:

> The appellant provided the appellate court with the appropriate standard of review: "an abuse of discretion." However, the appellant reached the wrong application of this legal standard. It was not an abuse for the trial court to grant custody of the minor child to his father, who has historically been the child's primary custodial parent. Therefore, there has been no abuse of discretion and the judgment should be affirmed.

D. FORMAT

The prescribed rules for word count and page length may differ for an appellee brief. Never exceed limits on word count or page length.

PRACTICE POINTER

Make a checklist to ensure compliance with all requirements of your jurisdiction for an appellee brief.

104. Georgia Court of Appeals Rules, Rule 23(b)(2).

E. HOW TO APPROACH THE RESPONDING OR APPELLEE BRIEF

It is both difficult and easy when you represent the appellee.

It is difficult to distinguish case law and authorities your opponent presented in his brief while simultaneously persuading the appellate court the judgment is sound. In a way, you must avoid over-responding to the appellant argument while at the same time effectively dealing with his or her arguments. That is the hard part.

But the job is also easier when you are the appellee. This is particularly true in family law matters.

Appellate courts apply broad discretion in reviewing family law issues. The reviewing court is loath to involve itself in intimate, personal skirmishes between formerly intertwined romantic actors. As much as the odds are against you as the appellant, the review court is firmly in your favor as the appellee.

Use the inherent bias against family law appeals and favorable odds to affirm the judgment.

Let's discuss the proper approach when you are supporting the judgment of the trial court.

F. HOW TO RESPOND TO THE APPELLANT'S BRIEF

The common dilemma for brief writers is how to address and respond to the appellant brief. You may believe, after first reading your opponent's brief, it is a complete waste of your time to respond. You are likely to be frustrated with your opponent's "spin on the case," particularly when you were trial counsel.

Or you may feel a response weakens your argument by even acknowledging your opponent's brief. But it is not a sign of weakness to file a response to points raised by the appellant.

Use your brief as an opportunity to persuade the appellate court of *how the trial judge got it right* by demonstrating directly the weakness in the appellant's argument.

Judge Hamilton of the federal fourth circuit notes the best briefs address "head-on the opponents' best argument, best responsive argument, best supporting case law or statutory authority."[105] If these authorities are missing in your brief, then the reviewing court may draw negative conclusions.

Judge Parker of the Second Circuit observes:

> I would also like to recommend that all advocates distinguish contrary authority, even in their opening brief. If there is bad precedent out there for your case, you can assume your adversary will cite it to us, or we will independently find it. If the first time I see an adverse case is in the answering brief, then my initial reaction is that the appellant does not have a good explanation as to why that case is inapposite. While a response in the reply brief may dispel this initial impression, it may not. Therefore, by failing to mention contrary precedent in the opening brief, the advocate makes that precedent weightier than it perhaps should be.[106]

The wisdom here is to confront your opponent's arguments. You do not need to dispel "all" all of his or her arguments, but attack any major components in your appellee brief.

Weigh your opponent's arguments carefully and determine which arguments are "major" and require an effective response.

It is never a bad idea to read and understand every case the appellant cited in his or her brief. You may find the appellant's use of case law is off point, thereby giving you an opportunity to destroy the credibility of your opponent's brief.

Practice Pointer

Always directly confront your opponent's strongest arguments.

Here is how to *not* utilize your opponent's argument in your responding brief.

105. Mary Beth Beazley, A Practical Guide to Appellate Advocacy 112 (4th ed. 2014) (quoting Judge Hamilton).

106. *Id.*, quoting Judge Parker.

BAD EXAMPLE[107]

The appellant argued that *Renert* applies to the facts in the present case. The appellant argues in his brief that *Renert* stands for the proposition . . .

In contrast, here are two good example of an appropriate manner to dispel your opponent's major arguments.

GOOD EXAMPLE 1

The appellant's argument that *Renert* applies to the fact here is inapposite. *Renert* never addressed the secondary income of the mother. . . .

GOOD EXAMPLE 2

Renert does not apply to the facts in the present matter for two reasons. First . . .

The key is to distinguish arguments your opponent made in his opening brief with contrasting case law.

Or demonstrate how the facts do not apply to the authorities presented by your opponent. This is a common occurrence. Use distinguishing facts to undercut your appellant's argument.

G. THE USE OF NEGATIVE AUTHORITIES

Confront negative authorities.

But do not start your brief with a contrast of negative authorities. Research shows dealing first with opposing viewpoints may decrease persuasive value.

107. Examples are adopted from Mary Beth Beazley, A Practical Guide to Appellate Advocacy 113 (4th ed. 2014).

Focus first and foremost on supporting the judgment of the lower court with your own authorities. Thereafter, confront negative authorities by demonstrating how your matter differs to the case law presented in your opponent's brief.

H. THE APPELLANT'S INCOMPLETE PICTURE

A common issue in family law appeals is that your opponent's brief does not articulate the complete picture in the trial court. In other words, your opposing party is "cherry picking" from the judgment in his or her brief to support his or her argument.

For example, take a custody matter, where the trial court awards custody to the mother. The father then appeals.

In his brief, the father argues the trial court improperly relied upon the report of the appointed guardian ad litem. The appellant brief extensively cites to precedents holding that a trial judge must reach his or her own independent judgment in awarding custody.

The reality is your opponent's brief fails to point out numerous pertinent "findings of fact" where the judge clearly demonstrates her or her reasoning supporting the judgment. These facts are:

1. Mother was historically the primary custodial parent.
2. Mother stayed home with the children for the past ten years.
3. Per the temporary orders of the parties, the mother had been granted primary custody of the children.

Let's expand how to handle your opponent's brief by using our prior *Renert* example:

> The appellant's reliance on *Renert* does not apply to the facts in the present matter for three reasons. First, the mother was historically the primary custodial parent of the children. Second, the mother stayed home with the children for the past ten years. And third, the temporary orders granted the mother primary custody of the children.

By pointing out the pertinent facts ignored by your opponent, you are providing a more accurate picture for the appeals court. You want appellate judges to think, "Oh that was the basis for the judgment," for the appellee to receive an affirmance of the trial court's judgment.

I. WATCH YOUR USE OF TONE

Never be disrespectful to your opponent. Always refrain from abusive attacks on opposing counsel in your appellee brief.

This is difficult in family law matters fought over many years, numerous court appearances, and deteriorating relationships between all parties, including counsel.

PRACTICE POINTER

Never make it personal in any brief.

Be mindful that appellate practice is not a contest to determine if you are more honest and honorable than your opponent. Do not let it become personal.

It is not your purpose to demonstrate to the appellate court how your opponent is a "bad apple." Keep in mind your focus is on the law—highlight the credibility of your argument, not the unworthiness of your opponent.

J. OKAY, FINE. BUT THEN HOW TO HANDLE THE OFF-BASE OPPONENT

There are subtle ways to make points that are appropriate. For example, it is perfectly appropriate to label an argument as being *incorrect*, *wrong*, or *fatally flawed*.

But avoid labels such as *deceptive*, *misleading*, *shocking*, or *absurd*. Never overhype it.

Allow the facts and the record to speak for themselves.

If you believe evidence produced by an opposing witness is entirely unreliable, you can still make an entirely respectful argument.

Here are two examples of how and how not to handle this situation.

> In summary, the husband failed to produce sufficient evidence of the wife's infidelity to grant a divorce under fault grounds. His "proof" was only a single phone record from an alleged ex-boyfriend to his wife on the occasion of her fiftieth birthday. There was nothing more produced. In fact, the wife credibly testified he was an old friend who shared the same birthday. Thus, the husband's evidence was insufficient for the lower court to grant the husband's divorce on the grounds of adultery. And therefore, the lower court's judgment of divorce on no faults grounds should be affirmed.

In contrast, here is what to avoid:

> In summary, the husband clearly suffers from paranoia and delusions that resulted in a ridiculous bogus claim of his wife's infidelity. He claims only that a single phone record from a college friend from years ago, who shared the same birthdate with the wife, was evidence of a torrid affair. This only showcases the extreme paranoia of the husband and is not substantial evidence of an affair that the wife specifically and credibly denied having. In fact, she testified she had not even seen her friend in twenty years. The husband's claim is patently and simply ridiculous! Therefore, the lower court's judgment of divorce on no fault grounds should be affirmed.

In the first and proper example, you did not indulge in personal attacks against the husband. Rather, you stuck to the facts and the law. You refrained from engaging in a personal attack against your opponent. It is much easier for the reader of your brief to "nod" in agreement.

While in contrast, the second argument, although perhaps accurate, has your reader thinking you have gone too far. Your attack on your opponent diminishes the power of your persuasion. The first example makes the point with zero risk of offending the reader of the brief.

The rule of refraining from personal attacks extends to pro se litigants and his or her briefs. When you are confronted with a pro se brief, the rules you follow in producing your appellee brief remain the same. Never engage in the "personal."

Practice Pointer

Treat a pro se writer of an appellant brief the same as you would treat a brief written by experienced counsel.

If you are careful to focus your appellee brief on supporting the lower court's judgment, contrast the arguments of your opponents with facts and case law and write in a professional, nonpersonal matter, your end product is an effective appellee brief.

There is one more possible brief to write. Let us turn our attention to the reply.

14 The Purpose of the Reply Brief: How? When? Why? And Ten Commandments

A. PURPOSE

The reply brief is the only written opportunity to respond to the appellee's brief. You may have an opportunity to respond to your opponent's arguments at oral argument, but the "reply" brief is a chance to directly counter what your opponent argued in response to your initial brief.

The filing of a reply is a permissive right in most, if not all, jurisdictions. So the decision for you is whether to file a reply.

Here is an example of one reply brief rule:[108]

> The appellant or other moving party may file a reply brief within twenty (20) days after the filing of a brief by the appellee or other adverse party. Except as otherwise provided in subsections (d) and (e), no party may submit any further or supplemental brief or postargument memorandum, or other communication of any kind, without the prior approval or direction of the Court or a justice thereof upon motion in

108. Rhode Island Rules of Appellate Procedure Rule 16.

accordance with Rule 28. Nothing in this rule shall prevent the making in any case, of a special order by the Court in regard to the time for filing any briefs.

B. TIMING

The time to draft and write a reply is shorter than all other briefs. This is the universal rule. If you are pressed for time, then file a motion for an extension of time. But keep in mind a reply brief is not required, so it is likely you will not be afforded a liberal extension of time.

C. CROSS APPEAL

The general rule in cross appeals is the party who filed the first notice of appeal is designated as the appellant. Thus, if you file the notice of appeal before your opponent, you are designated as the appellant and required to file the opening brief.

The party who filed the second notice of appeal is the appellee or respondent and required to file the responding or appellee brief.

D. FORMAT AND REQUIREMENTS

The format is the same as other briefs, but the required content is significantly less. For example, the reply requires a table of contents with page references, a table of cases, statutes, and other authorities cited, with references to the pages of the brief where they are cited.[109]

E. CONTENT

The purpose of the reply brief is different than the appellant brief. It is as its name suggests: to reply—to answer—to points by the appellee brief only.

109. Massachusetts Rule of Appellate Practice Rule 16.

A reply brief is a critical opportunity to refute the appellee's arguments. It provides you with the last word on the matter. It is never a bad opportunity for your client to have the last written word.

PRACTICE POINTER

Do not use the reply brief to repeat your arguments when your opponent failed to respond to them in the responsive brief.

F. WHEN NOT TO FILE

There might be times when a reply brief may not be necessary.

One example is when your opponent fails to raise any new issues. A second example is when you have addressed all of the issues in your appellant brief. A third example is when your opponent submitted a brief seriously deficient in every shape, form, and way. This is more than just disliking your opponent's argument or not agreeing with any points made. Think of the old Talking Heads song: this is literally when your opponent has "stopped making sense."

> *"Stop making sense, stop making sense . . . stop making sense, making sense."*
>
> —Talking Heads

Back to our paranoid husband from our last chapter as an example.

The paranoid husband, now pro se, submits a brief barely meeting the required format. It is essentially a diatribe against his ex-wife. He writes the following:

> This Honorable Court, by the powers thrust upon herself by the God almighty himself, knows that my wife has been sleeping around since the beginning of time, and I thereto as a result should not have to pay child support.

You get the general idea. In the instances where the brief is too incomprehensible to afford a response, skipping the reply brief is appropriate.

G. TEN COMMANDMENTS FOR REPLY BRIEFS

Use the following Ten Commandments to help you master the writing of an effective reply brief.[110]

COMMANDMENT 1 "When You Are the Appellant, You Almost Always File a Reply Brief"

You do not lose points for failing to file a reply, but you miss an opportunity to gain points. Adhere to the appellate rule to take every opportunity allowable by the rules to persuade the appeal court.

COMMANDMENT 2 "Your Reply Brief Is a Direct Answer to Your Opponent's Brief"

Never forget the basic purpose of a reply brief is *to respond only to the appellee*. A reply brief is not a condensed version of your appellant brief. Nor should it be a repetitive version of your opening brief. Get to the heart of your opponent's major points and dissect them.

COMMANDMENT 3 "Leave Out Your Weak Arguments in Your Reply Brief"

Your reply brief highlights the strongest points of your argument. Leave out any of your weaker arguments.

As U.S. Supreme Court Justice Oliver Wendell Holmes once stated: "Strike for the jugular, and let the rest go."[111]

110. These commandments are adapted in part from: Damon Thayer, *How to Write an Effective Reply Brief*, PRETRIAL PRACTICE & DISCOVERY. (American Bar Association, February 6, 2012).

111. OLIVER WENDELL HOLMES, SPEECHES 77 (Little, Brown, and Company, 1934).

COMMANDMENT 4 "Your Reply Brief Focuses on What Is Critical in the Appellee's Brief"

Your reply brief is an answer to the critical arguments made by your opponent, only. It is not a refutation of everything your opponent got wrong. Less is more.

As Robert Stern states:

> The reply should not attempt to deal with every conceivable error or omission in the appellee's brief which appellant is in a position to criticize. Nothing is more boring and less persuasive than a page by page, or point by point, attempt to rebut every inaccuracy, no matter how inconsequential. The reply should concentrate on what is significant.[112]

COMMANDMENT 5 "Maintain Credibility in Your Reply to the Court"

Always maintain credibility with the appellate court. Continue to be fair with all facts, both positive and negative. Apply the law to support your case in a credible manner.

Your duty to remain candid is amplified when you are writing the last word. Last words face closer scrutiny in any reply brief.

COMMANDMENT 6 "Provide Your Theory of the Case Again"

Your appellant brief has a theme—your theory of the case. The legal reasoning is applied to the set of facts supporting your argument and the result you request. Your theory of the case takes center stage in the beginning of your reply brief to provide greater emphasis to your argument.

---

112. Scalia & Garner, Making Your Case 73 (quoting Robert Stern).

COMMANDMENT 7 "Do Not Be Boring in Your Reply Brief"

Use your writing skills to engage your reader with the last word. For example, try memorable phrasing and utilize analogies and/or metaphors. Use your creativity and your personal touch.

But do not get too carried away with your literary prowess. Sometimes, the risk of creativity may not be worth the possible reward.

COMMANDMENT 8 "Make Your Reply Brief "Brief""

Do not feel compelled to write the reply brief maximum length allowed by your local rules. Rather, write only what is necessary. The appeals court sets only *maximum page or word counts, not minimums.*

Stop when you have stated what needs to be written.

COMMANDMENT 9 "Pay Attention to the Details in Your Reply Brief"

When drafting your reply brief, be careful when you begin to paraphrase or summarize to not change the meaning of your prior statements in your appellant brief. You run the risk of leaving your assertions unsupported and weakening your original argument in your opening brief.

Likewise, avoid errors on record or case citations.

COMMANDMENT 10 "Inform the Court of Exactly What You Want, Again"

Conclude your reply brief with your request for relief similar to how you closed your appellant brief. Be specific and ask the appeals court for exactly what you are seeking.

Follow these Ten Commandments, understand the importance and purpose of a reply brief, and write effective last words.

And now that the writing is complete, we turn our attention to what comes next: oral argument.

Oral Argument: What to Expect 15

The brief is finally done. The Record Appendix and related submissions are timely filed. You read the appellee brief. The reply brief is written and submitted. You feel you are now finished. You put it aside. But the fun is about to start. A few months or so, maybe more, maybe less if the matter is an expedited appeal, you receive the notice: the date and time of oral argument.

A. WILL THERE BE ORAL ARGUMENT?

Oral argument is a critical component of the appellate process. Discuss with your client the potential oral argument and the costs of preparation and the argument itself. Clients should understand the additional legal work necessary for a successful oral presentation.

But the first question to answer is whether your client is even afforded the opportunity. The rules of your local jurisdiction determine whether your appeals court grants oral argument.

In Illinois, for example, oral argument is rarely granted when one of the parties is pro se. Further, it is not granted unless requested on the cover of the appellant's or the appellee's brief.[113]

Some jurisdictions allow the parties to submit a decision on the "papers," but the appellate court may still direct the case to be argued.

PRACTICE POINTER

Know the rules of oral argument at the beginning of your written brief preparation.

B. A BRIEF WRITER SHOULD FAVOR ORAL ARGUMENT

As a general rule, you want an oral argument in your case.

The major exception is if you represent the appellee. When you are the appellee, you are looking to simply affirm the decision. Almost always, the less discussion about facts and law, the more advantageous for your client.

In addition, most family law appeals end with an affirmance. You do not want to provide the opposing side with an additional opportunity to persuade the appellate court how wrong the trial court got the matter.

Also, if your opponent submitted to the appeals court an ineffective brief, then you want to avoid providing another opportunity in the appellate court. If your state affords the opportunity to "opt out" of an oral argument, then almost always when you represent the appellee you want to do so.

In contrast, when you are the appellant, you want every single opportunity allowable to persuade the appeals court of the power of your argument. If your state permits you the ability to request oral argument, then do so.

Let's examine how to handle the appeals court discretion in granting oral argument by returning for a moment to our brief

113. Illinois Rules of Appellate Procedure 352(a).

writing to show that oral argument must be within your consideration during drafting.

C. WHEN YOU REPRESENT THE APPELLANT

Frame the case for your readers by pointing out the importance, beyond your client's interest, for a better opportunity to be granted oral argument. Take the following example.

The parties were married for only three weeks and the trial court awarded alimony for a period of one year to the opposing party. Argue the brevity of the marriage precludes an alimony award. Win or lose, an appellate decision would be applicable to all short-term marriages and not just your client's interest.

D. WHEN YOU REPRESENT THE APPELLEE

Conversely, when you represent the appellee, your job is to keep the case "vanilla" in your response to the reviewing court. Think of it as the "nothing to see here, folks" brief.

You want to frame the case to indicate:

1. There was no error.
2. Any error was harmless.
3. This is not a significant error.

Take our example of a child custody appeal.

The trial court awarded custody to your client, the mother, who is the primary custodial parent. However, the guardian ad litem recommended a shared parenting plan for the parties.

Your opponent argues the trial judge improperly ignored the recommendations and conclusions in the report.

This is the classic "abuse of discretion" argument.

Your job is to argue the great discretion trial judges are afforded in custody matters and how it was not an abuse of discretion to not implement the recommendations in the guardian ad litem report.

E. GENERAL PROCEDURE RULES OF ORAL ARGUMENT

The procedure for oral argument is the following.

1. Notice of Argument

The appellate court sends a notice of the time and place for your oral argument. To avoid conflicts, many appellate courts contact you in advance to schedule the date.

Once the oral argument is scheduled, the appeals court sends a formal notice of argument, which requires a reply by e-mail or by mail. The response requires the name of the attorney who will present oral argument for your client.

Generally, a request for postponement of the argument, after notice by the appellate court, must be made by motion filed reasonably in advance of the date fixed for hearing.

A compelling reason is necessary to reschedule the date for oral argument. Some appeals courts reschedule only for "grave cause."

2. Time Allowed

Most appeals courts allow approximately fifteen minutes for oral argument. Some state supreme courts allow for additional time if there is a novel or complex issue.

If you believe additional time is necessary to present your argument, request it for "good cause" shown. But avoid a request for additional time, as it is highly unusual.

PRACTICE POINTER

Your time allowed for oral argument will go fast.

3. Timer and the Lights

When you are in the courtroom, there is a set of timers and/or lights indicating the passage of time during your argument. The set of timers, one facing the podium and one facing the bench, is operated by the appellate court's clerk and is started at the appellate court's indication or when counsel begins to speak.

For example, in one court, the green light is the "go light" and is on for the first thirteen and a half minutes of argument. A yellow light is the "caution light" and indicates one and a half minutes remaining. A red light is the "stop light" and indicates the end of the time allotted.

Once the red light appears, the timer begins to count how much time is over the allotted amount. Appellate judges require you immediately conclude the argument, unless actively engaged in responding to a question from the bench.

Be familiar with the appellate court's procedure, as timers and lights vary from jurisdiction to jurisdiction. Go watch oral arguments and get a feel for how the court conducts them.

Practice Pointer

Pay attention to time but pay more attention to the chief justice to dictate when you are out of time.

4. Recording and Microphones

Many appellate courts broadcast in some form and arguments are recorded.[114] Be cognizant of the microphone, as it is preset to amplify as well as record your argument.

Speak in a clear, distinct manner so your voice is audible to the justices and you are clearly recorded. Avoid having notes or materials touching the microphone since this interferes with the recording and it is distracting to the presiding judges.

5. Order and Content

The order is simple and follows the written briefing order. The appellant argues first. The appellee goes last.

Most appeals courts state you are not permitted to read prepared statements except portions of your brief.

114. The exception being federal courts.

6. Rebuttal Argument

What about rebuttal argument?

The practice of rebuttal argument varies, and many states do not permit it. Check with your local rule. Rebuttal is discussed in greater detail in the next chapter.

7. Cross Appeals

What if there is a cross appeal?

A cross appeal is argued in a single oral argument. For example, if you are the appellant, be prepared to argue against the cross appeal of the appellee in your presentation.

F. SPECIAL RULES

1. Accommodations

If you or your client need special accommodations (e.g., special seating or hearing devices), notify the clerk's office in advance of your hearing date. Never make the request at the last minute. Request the accommodation at the time the oral argument is scheduled by the appellate court clerk.

2. No Shows

What happens if your opponent does not show?

Suppose your opposing party is pro se. We will give the benefit of the doubt to your opposing counsel, who runs the risk of a serious malpractice and ethical issue for failing to appear for a client.

If the appellee fails to appear for argument, the appellate court generally proceeds and hears your argument. Likewise, if the appellant fails to appear, the appeals court may allow argument on behalf of your appellee client.

And what if no one shows up? If no one appears, then the case will likely be decided on the briefs, unless the appellate court otherwise orders.

3. No Oral Argument by an Attorney/Witness

At times, you, the family law advocate, may believe you are a witness to events rather than an advocate for an individual client. It is just the nature of the work we do. But keep in mind one ethical constraint found in appellate rules.

There is a prohibition for an attorney to take part in the argument of a case in which he or she has been a witness for his client, except by special leave of court.

Hopefully, this does not happen in your own case. All precautions must be taken against becoming a "witness" in the trial court below, but it is worth a reminder here.

Practice Pointer

Always avoid inserting yourself in a family law dispute where you could be considered a witness at every stage of the litigation.

4. Use of Exhibits

Some appellate courts allow physical exhibits to be used at oral argument. However, this is rarely done in practice. Avoid it.

Effectively use the power of your words to persuade rather than using a chart, which is likely to offend appellate jurists.

In the event you intend to use an exhibit, then make arrangements well in advance of your argument through the appeals court. You may find the court's clerk discourages you from doing so.

Now with an understanding of the expectations of oral argument, let's turn to its importance along with its objectives.

3. No Oral Argument by an Attorney-Witness

16 The Importance, Advantages, and Objectives of Oral Argument

A. IMPORTANCE OF ORAL ARGUMENT

You may be petrified of oral argument. You want to win. You really hate to lose. You may have a fear of failing. Your argument is in public. You just hate speaking in front of people under the glare of the spotlight.

There is great pressure to make an impeccable presentation for your client. A child's life may hang in the balance of your words and your ability to persuade a group of strangers.

You get the idea.

All of these feelings make the very notion of oral argument so nerve-wracking. But it is routine to be a little nervous, but as soon as you begin to speak, the nervousness almost always disappears. Once you start, words flow and you start to feel better.

Embrace the opportunity provided by oral argument. Do not let normal apprehension affect your ability to do your job.

Be confident and prepared when you step before the court for oral argument. Use this opportunity to further persuade the appeals court. Address any appellate questions. Remove the appeals court of any doubt in the logic in your argument.

Oral argument is critical and can make the difference in your case.

Take note that appellate court judges, appellate lawyers, and academics believe oral argument is an important element in the process of successfully appealing a case.[115]

In addition, Supreme Court justices agree with the importance of oral advocacy.

Former Chief Justice Charles Evans Hughes wrote that oral arguments can form impressions that "accord with the conviction which controls his final vote."[116]

Two decades later, Justice Robert Jackson echoed the sentiments of the former chief: "I think the Justices would answer unanimously that now, as traditionally, they rely heavily on oral presentations. . . . It always is of the highest, and often of controlling, importance."[117]

The late Justice Antonin Scalia initially believed oral arguments were nothing more than "a dog and pony show" before joining the bench.[118]

But after sitting for almost two decades, his belief changed: "things . . . can be put in perspective during oral argument in a way that they can't in a written brief."[119]

If Supreme Court justices believe oral argument is a critical component of an appeal, never underestimate it in your appellate practice.

Does this mean your compelling oral argument will change a judge's mind?

It may. It may not. But that is beside the point.

---

115. Timothy R. Johnson, *Oral Advocacy Before the United States Supreme Court: Does It Affect the Justices' Decisions?* 85 Wash. U. L. Rev. 457 (2007).

116. *Id.*

117. *Id.*

118. *Id.*

119. *Id.*

Your job is to take every opportunity afforded to make your argument.

And what happens if your matter is a close call?

Oral argument can make the difference. It can get your argument over the top because it provides information and perspective that briefs may not contain. It may address a lingering question of the appellate court. It may breathe life into an issue.

An answer at oral argument may be a decisive factor.

A successful oral argument can therefore mean everything for your client.

One more thought here for consideration.

The critical importance of oral argument is truer in "close call" family law appeals. Intimate and personal matters can require more than words on paper. A well-crafted oral argument with a face upon it may tip the scales in your client's favor.

PRACTICE POINTER

Never underestimate the importance of oral argument.

B. ADVANTAGES OF ORAL ARGUMENT

The advantage to oral argument is an opportunity to place issues in proper importance for the appellate court. To emphasize the "heart of the matter" by using your own words. For example, you may start your oral argument with something like:

> Your Honors, we have three major points that we have argued in our brief. To us, each one of these points is important is interrelated. However, the heart of our argument is found in our third point—the husband's inability to work, and if it may please the court, I would begin there. . . .

PRACTICE POINTER

View oral argument as your opportunity to provide a humanistic perspective to your legal argument.

In addition, oral argument is important because it is an opportunity to provide to the court additional information.

For example, when you are the appellee, oral argument allows you the opportunity to reply to positions contained within the appellant's reply brief.

Without oral argument, you do not have the ability to argue the meritless nature of your opponent's reply.

C. OBJECTIVES OF ORAL ARGUMENT

Let's discuss the objectives of oral argument.

The objective of oral argument is not just winning the appeal. That is too easy. To succeed at oral argument, understand the role it plays in the advocacy process.

D. THE SIX OBJECTIVES OF ORAL ARGUMENT

Here are the six major objectives of oral argument.

1. Objective 1: To Answer All Questions and Remove All Doubt

Archibald Cox, Solicitor General of the United States under Presidents John F. Kennedy and Lyndon Johnson, explained that the role of the brief is to give the Court the ammunition to decide the case in your favor, while the role of oral argument is to persuade the judges to do so.[120]

Your first objective is to answer any questions the appellate court may have with your argument.

If you represent the appellee, refute major points raised in the appellant's reply brief. Keep in mind oral argument is your only chance to do so. For example, you may wish to state the following:

> If it pleases the court, I would like to start by addressing the reply brief's argument that the husband was not covered on the health insurance plan of the wife. First, the plan documents stated . . .

120. Appellate Practice in Federal and State Courts § 11.02.

Your objective here is to be direct, clear, and ready and able to answer any questions regarding the law, the facts, and to refute your opponent's arguments while doing so.

2. Objective 2: To Reinforce the Argument and Logic of Your Brief

Reinforce the substantive points made in your brief. Use your oral argument as an opportunity to reinforce the main points of your logic, mixed with the human factor of what you are asking the court to do.

Try this:

> May it please the court.
>
> My client, the primary caregiver, is seeking the prompt return of her child from Italy. The lower court has made an unfortunate but a legal error by improperly applying the wrong legal standard of removal to the facts in this matter. In short, it was not within the best interest of the parties' four-year-old to be allowed to remove to Italy with her father. . . .

The example nicely summarizes your argument, adds a human element, and provides clear guidance of what you are seeking from the court.

3. Objective 3: Address Your Theme

Your brief contains a theme.

Now is the time to return to your theme to make clear to the appeals court why your argument leads to the result you are requesting.

Leave the rostrum knowing the appeal court understands your theme: win, lose, or draw.

4. Objective 4: To Demonstrate You Are Thoughtful and Correctly Applied the Facts to the Law

Provide some "gravity" to the power of your oral argument.

You achieve this objective by the quality of your presentation. Show the panel you thought carefully and considered all important facts and the applicable case law.

Make it evident your argument is both thoughtful and proper. Leave your appellate panel thinking something must be done—when you are for the appellant—and nothing further to do—when you are for the appellee.

5. Objective 5: Show Your Likeability and Fairness

Demonstrate your likeability to the appellate court, mostly by your manner. Again, your objective is for the appellate court to "believe" you and your argument. A likeable person is likewise more believable.

Achieve this objective by connecting with the appellate judges by the power of your presentation and professional manner.

Be even-handed in your approach.

Keep in mind family law courts are courts of "equity," of fundamental fairness. You are asking the appellate court to review an equitable decision.

Show the panel you considered the converse—the other side of the street. And even with the strongest light shined upon your opponent's argument, your argument is reasonable, correct, and ultimately the fair result.

6. Objective 6: Never Miss a Thing

Your objective starts before you begin your opening statement. Know the record, the facts, and the law "cold." There should not be a question, a "factoid," a point of law you did not consider beforehand during your preparation, even if this requires additional time to prepare for your oral argument, some months after you put the matter down.

Indicate to the panel you know your stuff. It gives the panelists a sense of the depth of your knowledge and the completeness of your argument.

Now that we have set the bar high with our objectives for oral argument, let's see how we meet and exceed them in the next chapters.

Preparing for Oral Argument 17

Great oral advocacy is a skill only partially learned. Let's face it, to a certain extent, it is either in your genetic code or is acquired through lots and lots of practice. But well-thought-out and considerable preparation makes an effective advocate regardless of your skill level.

A. BE PREPARED AND THEN BE PREPARED AGAIN

There is no substitute for complete and thorough preparation for your oral argument. Preparation controls your nerves and instills confidence to make your arguments forcefully with sufficient support to the record. You preparation will allow you to handle with ease questions from the appellate panel. This last part is true because if you properly prepare, you know the record better than the judicial panelists and can anticipate the majority of questions you are asked.

PRACTICE POINTER

Your preparation instills the confidence necessary for an effective oral argument.

Be the advocate most familiar with the facts, a new statute, or recent case law. Demonstrate to the appellate court authority and command.

Think of a great basketball player such as Michael Jordan, who took control late in the fourth quarter of close games. Why?

Because he possessed greater command of the game than all the other players.

Make it your goal: "To be like Mike."

So, wait, how and what do you prepare?

Personal style dictates how you prepare for oral argument. The following principles are necessary for effective preparation for all oral arguments.

B. KNOW THE RECORD

Learn and know the record "cold."

There is absolutely no shortcut or excuse for not having a complete understanding of the record within the lower court. A failure to possess a thorough understanding of the record causes you considerable strife and undermines any argument before the appellate panel.

Further, maintain an organized understanding of the record. You want to quickly find material at any time.

Be in a position to promptly address a critical fact within the record, if it comes up at oral argument. Only by remaining organized and understanding the record can you handle all questions from the appeals court.

C. ORGANIZE YOUR OWN RECORD

Organize the record to assist your preparation.

Create an index and tab your materials for use during your preparation for oral argument. By staying organized from the inception of your oral argument preparation, you save valuable time so you can focus on being fully prepared when it is time to go before the appellate panel.

D. KNOW YOUR CASES

Understand all the cases cited in your brief. There is a significant passage of time from the submission of your written brief until your oral argument. The passage of time can lead to forgetting important points in case law that you have relied upon in your brief.

Use the time leading up to your oral argument wisely by reviewing your pertinent cited cases.

Expect to be challenged at oral argument.

A mastery over your case citations is necessary to ensure command over the law in the matter. What is the best way to avoid rereading every case?

Think back to law school. Think of when you spent vast time reading and summarizing cases. What did you need to remember? The pertinent facts. The major legal issues. And what proposition the case stands for.

Follow the same methodology as you prepare for oral argument.

Review the important cases you cited. Recall the facts, the legal issues, and the holding in each case. Keep the case law organized in your preparation materials.

E. KNOW *YOUR* CRITICAL FACTS

Know *all* your *critical* facts of your case.

I'll write it again: family law matters are intricately connected to the specific, individual facts of each case. It is imperative to never lose sight of critical facts when you are arguing about the legal principles of applicable case law and statutes.

PRACTICE POINTER

Do not rely on a junior associate for your understanding of the facts. Be personally familiar with all factors of your case.

Appellate courts pay attention to individual facts in family law appeals more than you may realize. The appellate court may raise a fact with you in oral argument on which the appellate judges are unclear and believe makes a difference in prior case law.

Be ready to respond with your complete mastery of all the facts contained in the record.

Return to your facts during your oral argument preparation and highlight key points.

In the same manner you prepare your critical cases and statutes, create a guide to quickly locate all important facts.

F. OUTLINE YOUR ARGUMENT

An oral argument outline is an essential part of your preparation. Consider using a graphical representation like a flow chart or a mind map of your argument that fits on one page.

PRACTICE POINTER

Use your brief outline to formulate your outline for oral argument.

Keep your oral argument outline to a manageable length by eliminating minor issues, which are unlikely to be addressed by the appellate court. For example, the massive disagreement on what to name the family pet of the parties. You get the idea.

Do not fill your outline with too many materials from your brief, such as full-length court opinions or trial exhibits. Limit your outlined material to case law summaries and key factual points from your Record Appendix.

Let's next discuss how to remain on major points to create an effective argument outline.

PRACTICE POINTER

Outstanding preparation for oral argument makes the difference between an average presentation and a presentation your client deserves.

G. MAJOR POINTS

Put away the briefs, the case law, the summarization of the facts, financial statements, guardian ad litem reports, and notes made regarding the case.

Instead, create brief sentences on only the important points of your argument. Focus with precision on arguments to return to when confronted with a battery of questions from the appellate panel.

Memorize these major points. It should not be difficult, as these points are the essence of your argument.

Once you prepare a draft outline of your argument, review all briefs, gather any further cases for review, and if necessary, make any additions on important concepts only to your draft outline.

If you find your outline to be far too long or cumbersome, then make revisions by eliminating excessive information and material.

H. USE A NOTEBOOK TO STAY ORGANIZED

Utilize a notebook to stay organized. A small three-ringed binder is sufficient. Use it for your outline and perhaps a few other key pieces of information, such as key case provisions from major case law and/or pertinent facts to have at the ready from your Record Appendix.

Place your closing and opening in your notebook. Use your notebook throughout your preparation.

I. DRAFT AN OPENING AND CLOSING

Include an opening and a closing in your outline of your preparation. Commit both to memory.

J. THE OPENING

The hardest part of public speaking is finding a compelling opener to engage your audience. The beginning of any oral argument is also compounded by your nerves.

A proper prepared opening provides you with the fuel to be comfortable and confident. A memorized opening eliminates the worry about what you are beginning with.

But do not read from a prepared text.

Confidently address your audience with your memorized opening and make eye contact as you speak. Engage your audience with a compelling argument from the start.

So what should an opening state?

Your opening consists of a very brief outline summary of the major issues to address with the appellate court. Take the following example.

> May it please the court.
>
> I would like to address three major issues today. First, how the lower court misapplied the child support guidelines. Second, how it failed to make sufficient findings for an alimony award. And third, why the marital property division was inequitable for the wife . . .

It is unlikely you reach all three topics before an appellate judge pounces on you with questions once you say the words *child support*.[121]

Be prepared regardless!

By setting forth at the outset what you hope to address, it can make the appellate judge's questions more directed on the topics in your argument you want to present. It is your attempt to steer the agenda. This strategy is not always successful but keeps your attention focused on the important points to argue.

Both you and your client may experience a sense of relief when you are able to cover each of the major topics in your argument.

K. HOW TO PREPARE YOUR OPENING

Prepare your opening argument by drafting one or two sentences articulating your major points. Try to imagine the one or two thoughts you need the appellate judges to be left with when you are finished.

---

121. In fact, in my last two arguments before the Massachusetts Supreme Judicial Court, I am reminded how the same distinguished jurist began asking me questions before I even could introduce myself to the panel.

Here is an example.

> The alimony statute is unconstitutional because it allows a judge to invalidate alimony awards prior to the passing of the Act.

In this example, you are signaling to the appeals court why the court should adopt your position in a single sentence.

PRACTICE POINTER

As part of your preparation, focus on developing a single sentence defining your argument.

One final point regarding your opening statement.

Avoid controversy. If and when you start with a controversial point, you invite more hostile questions from your appellate panel at the outset of your argument. Never an easy way to begin.

L. DRAFT A CLOSING

You want to end any oral argument on a high note. It is the last "word" and the last impression the appellate court has on both you and your argument.

You never know how the panel may go, but you may be afforded an opportunity to wrap up your argument.

Do not summarize all of your major points in your closing. Rather make one final demonstrative point and remind the appeals court again what your client is seeking.

Here is an example.

> In closing, the trial judge failed to consider all of the facts contained within Chapter 208 Section 34, and therefore, we ask the court to remand the matter to the trial court for further findings to consider all the factors enumerated by the statute and issue a revised proper property division. Thank you."

One other point. Avoid being overly dramatic with your closing.

This can be extraordinarily challenging when you are representing a mother who lost custody of a child to the other parent.

But recall who you are before.

You are not before a jury of laypeople, but instead presenting before a panel of cynical appellate court judges.

Your goal is to leave them with your argument to consider. The logic and reason of your argument is more powerful than your passionate plea to the appellate court.

M. READ DECISIONS OF THE APPELLATE JUDGES ON THE PANEL

It is a good to know your appellate panel. This means reading and reviewing key decisions in family law an appellate panelist has written. It gives a good sense of a judge's potential viewpoint on a particular subject.

Perhaps you have an alimony case and there is an appellate jurist who wrote the last two seminal cases on the topic in your jurisdiction. Guess who's writing the opinion in your case? Pay particular attention to that appellate jurist's questions.

N. VIEW ORAL ARGUMENTS

View oral arguments as part of your preparation process.

Most professional speakers get an advance look at the room where they are speaking. You should too. It provides comfort to understand the layout of the room, where people sit and where they stand during oral argument. Comfort brings familiarity, which brings you confidence.

PRACTICE POINTER

Be familiar with the room where you are arguing.

Just as reading briefs on family law subjects, it is helpful to watch appellate arguments focused on a family law matter. This provides an idea of how the appellate court judges view the subject matter and the type of questions asked, and it gives you a good idea of what to expect in your own argument before the court.

Some states, such as Massachusetts, through the Suffolk University Law School project, have every Massachusetts Supreme Judicial Court argument available for viewing since the project began in 2005.[122]

Check your local jurisdiction. Or visit the appellate court to watch a family law argument. States list a schedule of oral arguments on appellate websites. Check the table provided at the end of this book to find your local appellate website.

O. STAY CURRENT WITH CASE LAW AND STATUTORY CHANGES

Never arrive to the appeals court and find your key case overturned. Or that the appellate court decided to take up a similar issue in another matter. Always update your legal research a few days before your oral argument.

Go even further. Read all family law decisions issued after your brief is submitted to remain current on the law. Check the docket on those cases as well. You never know what you may find helpful. Staying current with case law also allows an understanding as to how the appellate court is thinking about issues in family law cases.

PRACTICE POINTER

Register with the appeals court of your jurisdiction to receive all decisions issued or have a system in place to receive all opinions as adjudicated.

P. CONDUCT A MOOT COURT FOR YOUR CASE

Conduct a moot court for your case.

It is great preparation for oral arguments to have interested colleagues interrogate you on issues you are addressing before the actual appeals court. A moot court brings out unanticipated problems to correct before the actual argument.

122. Go to http://www.suffolk.edu/sjc/. You can view the author's argument online.

Find lawyers unsympathetic to your argument and who practice family law so there is familiarity with the law in question. Ask them to read the briefs on the matter.

Make the mock court as real as possible. Time the event. Use the same beginning (all rise), middle (timing), and end of the actual oral argument. Create the tension felt at oral argument.

Finally, consider videotaping the proceedings. The use of reviewing videotape is difficult to watch but reminds you of the strengths and weaknesses of your case—and what you need to work on as you complete your preparation for your oral argument.

In closing, oral argument goes by very quickly. It is the culmination of weeks of preparation in only a few action-packed minutes. But when you properly prepare, it provides the confidence to be engaging, compelling, and persuasive. You may even find your argument is fun![123]

---

123. After your oral argument, give yourself the day off. You will be "spent" from your preparation and you deserve it!

Presenting at Oral Argument 18

There are fundamental rules to follow when arguing before an appellate panel. Here are tips to make your argument successful.

A. DRESS FOR SUCCESS

Acknowledge the importance of oral argument by presenting the best possible optics. The right "power outfit" can serve as a big confidence booster.[124]

Do not believe me? Well, there is even some proof.

In a 2012 study published in the *Journal of Experimental Social Psychology*, subjects who donned doctors' lab coats scored higher on attention-related tasks than did those who did not.[125]

---

124. Sarah Stebbens, *How to Dress for Success*, REAL SIMPLE, https://www.realsimple.com/beauty-fashion/clothing/dress-for-success-0#dress-for-success.

125. *Id.*

According to a survey of business leaders published by the Center of Professional Excellence at York College of Pennsylvania, two-thirds said when it comes to getting ahead, image makes a major impact.[126]

There is nothing to lose and everything to gain by putting your best and appropriate fashion foot forward for oral argument.

B. USE STAFF FOR CLIENT LOGISTICS

If family, friends, or clients are coming to the oral argument, use staff members to deal with the logistics. Avoid distractions. Warn your client you cannot be distracted on the day of oral argument and let them know in advance. Meet with them the week before and let them share their thoughts. On the day of oral argument, stay focused on your presentation.

PRACTICE POINTER

Always arrive early for oral argument—at least ninety minutes before is a good rule of thumb.

Give yourself plenty of time so you are fully engaged. Make a stop at the restroom before entering the courtroom. Take a moment to remind yourself you are ready and your preparation is about to pay off.

Again, know your court's rules and practices for oral argument, as some clerks call the docket at the beginning of the session and you may miss roll call and not be allowed to argue.

Spend time thinking about your opening, the outline of what you want to argue, and how to close.

It is never a bad idea to watch other arguments before the appeals court while you wait for your turn to argue. Sitting quietly in the courtroom can actually be relaxing. It can give you the particular flavor of the type of panel you might be facing.

---

126. *Id.*

C. THE PODIUM

Do not bring a number of items with you to the podium. It distracts the appellate judges and makes you appear less than prepared. If you really are concerned you may need a document from your files, then bring an associate or an assistant to provide you the material.

The classic example is opposing counsel struggling to recall a fact and a clever associate finding what is missing for you, so when it is your turn, you can say something along the following:

> "May I address one fact not clear from my sister's argument? The husband was in fact married twice. The record for the first marriage is found in the Record Appendix on page 77. . . ."

PRACTICE POINTER

Be minimalistic in what you bring to the podium.

D. GO TIME

When it is your turn, take a deep breath, stand up, and go to the podium. Make some initial eye contact with the judges and start with the usual: "May it please the court."

If you ever have the good fortune of appearing before the U.S. Supreme Court, it is customary to start with "Mr. Chief Justice and may it please the court."

Many times, and if you have appeared before the appeals court in the past, the presiding judge greets you by your name.

Otherwise, if the court has not referred to you by name, then you add, "May it please the court. I am (your own name) for the appellant."

E. CONNECTION

Always attempt to connect with the appellate judges during your presentation. This is particularly important at the beginning, when you are answering the appellate court's questions and also at the end of your argument.

For example, when you are asked a question, look at the judge asking it when you are answering. Address the individual judge by name.

Be familiar with the correct pronunciation of each appellate judge's name. There is nothing more embarrassing than getting a judge's name wrong! Even worse, when you continuing doing so throughout your argument before the appellate court.

F. TERMINOLOGY

Use correct appellate court terminology.

Even if you are new, act like you have been there before or, at the very least, like you belong there. Fake it until you make it, so to speak.

Use the correct titles for appellate judges used by your local courts, which can depend upon which court you are before. Some are "judges" while other courts they are "justices."

Judges notice when you use incorrect terminology. It diminishes your credibility and therefore your argument.

G. AVOID THE CLOCK

Be aware of the time, but never look at your watch directly during your oral argument. It is a distracting habit during an oral argument. You risk offending an appellate judge who may notice.

Finally, when you reached the end of your time, do not try for any additional time unless the presiding judge allows you to answer or grants you additional time.

If your thought is incomplete, try the following:

> "I see the red light and realize I am out of time. May I just briefly complete my answer?"

H. BE PROFESSIONAL

Be professional at all times before the appellate court. Use your time wisely. Attempt to cover all the major points needed to make your argument. Be courteous and polite.

Resist the temptation of introducing your colleagues, your associate, and/or your intern. It unwisely takes the attention off the importance of your argument and is a time-waster. It is unnecessary and unappreciated by the reviewing court.

Appreciate the importance of your moment in the law by engaging in professional conduct.

I. THE USE OF HUMOR

Everyone likes to laugh. Everyone likes to be funny, if he or she can. Who does not appreciate a good joke or a wicked sense of humor? But humor has a place and an appropriate time. Do not tell prepared jokes. You are not a comedian. You are an advocate.

Here is a classic example from the Justice Scalia and Bryan A. Garner appellate book on arguing and persuasion:[127]

> In Roe v. Wade, an assistant attorney general for the state of Texas, who was arguing against two women lawyers, led with what he probably considered courtly Southern humor:
>
> "Mr. Chief Justice, and may it please the court, it's an old joke, but when a man argues against two beautiful ladies like this, they're going to have the last word."

Dead and awful silence. No one laughed in the audience. Those who witnessed it said that during an embarrassing silence, Chief Justice Burger just scowled rage at the advocate.[128]

J. REBUTTAL

In many courts, it is customary for you to request rebuttal time in advance, while other courts prohibit it. If you plan on using rebuttal time then reserve it at the beginning of your argument.

If rebuttal is afforded, make sure the timer or lights, depending which is used, are factored into your time in advance. Otherwise, the red light could signal the end of all your allotted time. Find out

---

127. Scalia & Garner, Making Your Case 187.
128. *Id.*

in advance from the appellate court's clerk how the timing system is operated.

If rebuttal is allowed by your local jurisdiction, reserve a couple of minutes for rebuttal, but not more than five minutes. Only two or three minutes are necessary for you to make a few strong ending points in response to the appellee's argument. For example, point out an important fact the appellee missed or a legal precedent contradicting a claim your opponent just made.

Rebuttal does not make a significant difference. You rarely gain ground, but do not give up the opportunity for the last words.

Let's next explore how to handle questions and various types of appellate panels you confront at oral argument.

19 How to Handle Questions, Common Occurrences, and Appellate Panels at Oral Argument

A. BE READY TO NAVIGATE THE APPELLATE COURT'S QUESTIONS

The key to oral argument is to anticipate the questions from the appellate panel. Be prepared and ready for the likely questions you are going to be required to answer.

Always answer the question you are actually asked. Listen and focus on exactly what the appellate judge is asking to effectively answer his or her question. From one former chief justice:

> If you are going to be able to intelligently answer a question, you must first listen to the question . . . It is surprising how often appellate advocates, just like many people in private conversation, seem to hear only part of the question, and respond to that part of

it that they had heard even though the answer they give may not be an adequate response to the entire question.[129]

How do you specifically handle questions?

Respond with a "yes" or "no." If necessary, explain further.

For example, "Yes, Your Honor, but in this matter the wife is capable of working full-time, which contrasts with . . ."

Or.

"No, Your Honor, unless we take into the history of earnings of the parties, which the trial court did not address . . ."

The point is you want an answer for the appellate court followed by an explanation and not an explanation first.

B. SOME ANSWERS TO AVOID

There are some forms of answers to avoid when you are before the appellate court. Here are two major responses to steer clear of when you argue:

1. **Avoid overhyping a response.**
   Do not engage in hyperbole. For example, "This is the greatest injustice in the history of the probate court system."
2. **Do not praise the appellate court for a question.**
   Refrain from praising the appellate court for thoughtful questions. For example, "You know, Your Honor, that is an excellent question." You are likely to be excited when you have anticipated a question and want to praise the appellate judge for asking what you are thinking. But your attempt at flattery may fall flat or even be offensive to a panel of hardened appellate judges.

129. SCALIA & GARNER, MAKING YOUR CASE 191 (quoting Hon. William H. Rehnquist).

C. HYPOTHETICALS

Hypothetical questions are asked at oral argument. Learn to embrace the hypothetical—even when it is off the wall. Try the following:

> **"Yes, I agree the husband should not have to pay alimony after he has passed away, but that is not the case in the present matter."**

As you prepare, ask yourself your own hypothetical questions to apply to your argument. By developing your own hypotheticals, you are able to handle these forms of questions from the appellate panel.

D. UNKNOWN ANSWERS

What if you do not know an answer to a question?

If you do not have an answer to a question, it is better to be honest and acknowledge your inability to answer the question. Try the following:

> **"I am sorry, Your Honor, but I do not know the answer. If it is acceptable to the court, I will provide the information by letter this afternoon."**

Another acceptable approach:

> **"Your Honor, I do believe the answer to the question is yes; however, I am not entirely certain on that point."**

PRACTICE POINTER

Never respond to a question from the appellate court with a guess.

Never guess. Never even try to guess. It is a better approach to be direct and candid with all of your responses to the appellate court—even those you do not know!

E. BE FLEXIBLE

Be flexible and be ready to adapt to what you are confronted with at oral argument. Never expect to "argue" your points in a sequential order. Expect the unexpected and be prepared to go where the appellate court leads you.

Be prepared for all of the following:

1. To speak with interruption from the bench
2. To speak without interruption from the bench
3. To speak with a limited number of questions
4. To speak with a limitless amount of questions

Have a game plan for all of these scenarios. Make your points regardless of the style of panel and be prepared to adapt to the appellate panel you are facing.

PRACTICE POINTER

Always listen very carefully to the court's questions and respond directly.

F. NEVER POSTPONE AN ANSWER TO A QUESTION

Never do the following:

> **"Your Honor, I'll address it later in my argument. Let me start with the issue of child support and we will return to custody later. . . ."**

Judges want answers to *the question* they are asking you.

View oral argument as you are there to serve the appellate panel. You are the waiter or the waitress serving up your logical argument to the hungry patrons on the appellate court.

Advocate by providing the appellate panel with direct responses to the information being sought.

Your answers are your advocacy.

The problem with being nonresponsive is it causes the appellate panel to think you lack an answer. It diminishes your argument.

Address *all* questions from the panel. Go where the court wants you to go!!!!

In summary, learn to embrace questions from the appellate court. Treat questions from appellate judges as your opportunity to validate your arguments. Your answers resolve issues troubling to the appellate judges and remove ambiguity with your argument. Questions confirm appellate judges are paying attention.

G. TYPES OF JUDGES/PANELS

Appellate panelists come in all shapes and sizes. Some are extraordinarily active while others are downright passive. Understand all the types of jurists you may encounter in your arguments.

Sometimes you encounter a recalcitrant appellate court judge whose questions are designed to demonstrate to the other panelists the weakness of your case. Hence, the difficult judge—so let's start there.

H. HOW TO HANDLE A DIFFICULT JUDGE

How do you handle the difficult judge?

First, display belief in your arguments. Be steady. Do not quiver, shake, or fidget. You can do this. Think of your client and why you are there. Stay focused upon making your argument.

Look the judge square in the eye and respond in a professional, but firm manner.

Recall your theme. Make your points in the context of the appellate judge's questioning.

> *"Don't raise your voice, improve your argument."*
>
> —Desmond Tutu

PRACTICE POINTER

No matter what, do not let the panelists see you sweat.

What do you do when the difficult judge repeatedly asks you the same question over and over again?

You do not want your time killed with the appellate panel. Use a polite way to get out of the repetitive loop. Consider trying the following:

> **"Your Honor, I believe the answer would be the same and I am unable to add anything further in response to your question. If I may, I would now address the issue of the husband's alimony. . . ."**

Likewise, a judge may be focused on only one part of your presentation and time begins to grow short for you to address other critical areas of your argument you want to highlight.

There, you must turn the appellate court's attention directly.

Remain polite, but assert some control to get your argument back on the right track. Try the following, only after responding to the last question:

> **"With the court's permission, I would like to turn now to . . ."**

Remind yourself *it is your argument.*

I. WHEN ONLY ONE POINT IS NECESSARY FOR YOUR ORAL ARGUMENT

Never feel pressured to make all three points of your argument, when only one major point is necessary. If it is necessary, explain to your client that the appellate court was focused on only one of the issues you had briefed. Thus, your other two points were made in your written submissions and are under consideration before the appellate court.

PRACTICE POINTER

Sometimes, one major point is enough to win your argument.

J. ALWAYS AVOID HOSTILITY

You may face not only a "difficult" judge, but also an entire panel hostile to you or your argument or both. Perhaps it is your tie? But it is more likely your argument rubbed a panelist or even a panel the wrong way. So, what do you do?

You must never reply in kind. Always avoid becoming hostile. Contain your anger. Never look annoyed. Remain patient with the appellate panel. Do not provide a further opportunity for the appellate panel to turn even more against you and your argument.

This may be difficult because you realize your well-crafted brief is for naught.

But in those moments, stay committed to your argument, and to your client. Return to your theme, make your points, and address directly the panel's questions.

Be comforted with this famous exchange.[130]

> A noted barrister, F. E. Smith, had argued at some length in an English court when the judge leaned over the bench and said: "I have read your case, Mr. Smith, and I am no wiser than I was when I started."
>
> To which the barrister replied, "Possibly not, My Lord, but far better informed."
>
> Smith, who later became a famous judge as the Earl of Birkenhead, could reportedly carry off such snappy rejoinders with impunity.

Do not emulate Mr. Smith, but be mindful of his sentiments to help you get through your own argument.

Something further to consider:

> *"Very often in everyday life one sees that by losing one's temper with someone who has already lost his, one does not gain anything but only sets out upon the path of stupidity. He who has enough self-control to stand firm at the moment when the other person is in a temper, wins in the*

130. Scalia & Garner, Making Your Case 199.

end. It is not he who has spoken a hundred words aloud who has won; it is he who has perhaps spoken only one word."

—Hazrat Inayat Khan, *Mastery through Accomplishment*

K. BEWARE OF CONCESSIONS

Be careful what points you concede at oral argument.

There are moments when conceding a minor point validates the integrity of your argument. But be careful to not concede a major point of your argument under the glare of the judicial spotlight.

Why?

Your concession gives away your case.

Stick to your argument. Avoid at all costs giving away a crucial fact. Be polite, but there is a limit to your courtesy with the appellate panel.

PRACTICE POINTER

Adhere to your theory of the case and do not concede it under any circumstances.

You may believe you are being reasonable in your response when you make a concession. Take the following example:

"Counsel, even if we agree with your argument the husband overpaid his alimony, does it really matter if we now remand the matter, now that the term of alimony has ended?"

But the answer must always be:

"Yes, Your Honor, *it does matter* and here is why. . . ."

The result has to matter. It must matter. If it does not matter, then you lose the case.

A judge may be seeking to test the validity of your argument.

Take another example.

You are defending a trial court's alimony judgment on the ground the trial judge considered all the major factors under the statute in fashioning an award of alimony.

Counsel for the husband contends alimony is unwarranted due to the large division of marital assets the wife received. You receive the following loaded inquiry from the appellate court:

> Counsel, surely you would agree with me if a person has received over ten million dollars of assets in a property division they have sufficient assets to enable them to support themselves independent from the other party and without any alimony?

Your mind thinks what a wonderful opportunity to demonstrate how I am a reasonable person. However, if you concede the point, you abandon the fundamental premise of your case: alimony is independent from the property division!

By being agreeable on this singular point, you allow the appellate panel to conclude your client did not need alimony. The matter ends. You end up with the following opinion:

> **"Counsel acknowledged at oral argument[131] due to the large grant of property division to the wife, she lacked the requisite need for alimony. We therefore remand this matter to the trial court for further findings based upon our decision."**

In the cozy comfort of your office, you regret being so "reasonable" with the appellate court.

So, what is your response to the loaded question from the panelist?

Try this:

> **"No, Your Honor, I do not agree with your premise based upon the facts of this case, and neither did the lower court, because the trial judge specifically addressed the amount of the property division and actually took into consideration in the award of alimony to the wife. . . ."**

131. The insult to the injury!

Never forget your essential purpose to argue and persuade the appellate court of the logic of your argument. Be careful with your politeness and reasonableness when it intersects with your purpose.

L. THE QUIET PANEL

Courts are very busy places. Appellate courts can be even busier places. They are the bakeries of the law distributing legal precedents instead of delicious "M&M" cookies. You may be the first argument of the day, the middle, or even the last. Your number is called and then you go.

You start. Nothing. You keep going.

You make it through your well-planned and memorized opening and the expected questions are not flowing from the appellate panel.

Last up, late in the afternoon and the panel is uninterested in the one family law case of the day.

Now what?

These are times to not think *and just do*. All of your preparation results in you having the law and the record down cold. Make your argument, focus on your theme, and go for it.

Move succinctly to each major point in your case.

Do not let your mind wander. Do not think the appellate panel is for you or against you. In these moments, be reminded of the words of the great Bill Belichick:[132] *Just do your job.*

Your focus upon your argument when confronted with the disinterested panel demonstrates to your client the best possible case was made to the appeals court.

M. INVITE QUESTIONS

Consider inviting questions from your quiet panel:

---

132. For the uninformed, the greatest coach in the history of the National Football League.

For example, state: "Unless the court has any further questions on the wife's inheritance, I will turn to the other items in the division of the marital estate."

This brings me to another strategic consideration.

N. LAND MINES

At times it is useful to include a "land mine" in an argument, just to see if it explodes. For example, you are before the appeals court on a custody removal matter and a recent decision issued in a neighboring state adopts a new standard for child custody removal.

The new standard is potentially beneficial to your client in your case before the appeals court. Point out, in the context of your argument, the other state's newly adopted standard, to check if there is any interest in adopting a new standard in your jurisdiction.

O. ALWAYS STOP WHEN YOU ARE AHEAD

Time limits are constraints upon the time you are allowed under the rules of the appellate court for oral argument. They are similar to word and page maximums contained in the rules for written briefs. And so likewise, there is no "minimum" amount of time given for your oral argument by the appeals court.

When you find yourself ahead, which is usually when the court is not pressing you or is seemingly agreeing with your argument, recognize it is time to conclude.

The actual time for oral argument is remarkably short. A brief argument can be enough. It is not a violation of any rule to use less time than allotted.

If you have nothing further to add for the appellate panel, then do not be afraid to quickly and quietly conclude your argument. If there are no further questions forthcoming, have the confidence to stop.

A good way to handle this situation is the following:

> **"If the panel has no further questions, I will stop here and rest on our submissions. Thank you."**

Or you can conclude with: "For all other issues, I rely on my brief."

Keep in mind the following.

> *Better to remain silent and be thought a fool than to speak and to remove all doubt.*
>
> —Abraham Lincoln

In closing, one author describes oral argument in the following precise way:

> Oral argument is like jazz. It is imperfect, unpredictable and risky, yet immediately personal and powerful.[133]

By committing to being fully prepared and understanding the goals of oral argument, you navigate your oral argument with ease and make music for all of your clients.

---

133. Alan L. Dworsky, The Little Book on Oral Argument (Hein, William S. & Company, Inc., 1991).

Aftermath: The Appellate Decision 20

Oral argument ended long ago. Appellate briefs and binders now sit atop the trial binder and exhibit books sitting ominously in the corner of your office gathering dust. When suddenly an e-mail appears in your smartphone's inbox and then there it is: the appeals court decision.

As you read, just as you reviewed the trial decision months ago, your heart races and pounds while you skip to the conclusion. You read it. You then read it again. You check which jurist wrote the decision. So this is it. You read it one more time more carefully.

You review the holding. You look at the issues the appeals judge examined. You look for key facts and critical holdings by the appellate court. You think back to your argument. You think how it played into the appellate court's decision. Is it right? Wrong?

Did we win? Did we lose? Neither? Is it over?

You think of your client. You think of all the hard work to reach this point.

You think again of the matter.

So this is justice.

What do I do now?

The appellate decision is certainly almost the end of the long judicial road. However, there are a number of outcomes in a family court appellate decision to examine after the issuance of the appellate decision. This final chapter is about what to do after receiving the appellate court's decision.

A. THE EFFECT OF THE DECISION

As you read your appellate decision, your natural appellate instinct, beyond determining the outcome upon your client, is the effect of the decision on family law in your local jurisdiction. There are two categories of appellate decisions: published or unpublished.

An unpublished decision affects the parties *in this matter only* with no precedential value on other future litigants in your local jurisdiction. Moving forward an unpublished decision can be cited, depending upon local rule *for persuasive value* only.

An unpublished decision is a determination of a lack of substantial question of law presented by your appeal. This is not to say your appellate decision when unpublished is meaningless.

The decision can be utilized to persuade a court in limited certain fact patterns. For example, take a child support guidelines matter involving part-time income earned from the car service Uber. Perhaps a future case involves similar facts involving similar part-time income and an application of the guidelines. If so, your case is cited for persuasive value.

Never think of an unpublished decision as a reflection on your appeal's quality. Rather, it is a limitation on how the appellate court views the matter when applied to future litigants.

Some matters are more unique to parties than in overarching legal principals. A victory for your client in an unpublished legal opinion returning custody to your client is a win regardless of the type of appellate decision.

In contrast, a published opinion issued by the appeals court serves as binding precedent and can be cited by future litigants to the appellate court in your jurisdiction. For you, this can be a win-win. A win for your client and a victory for all similarly situated litigants in the future!

B. THE DECISION VS. MANDATE

You receive first the appellate decision. Be aware the decision itself does not transfer jurisdiction of the matter back to the local court. You will need to wait for the "mandate" from the appellate court. The mandate transfers jurisdiction back to the local court. Knowing the difference will allow you to advise your client as to where to seek further remedies. For example, enforcement of the judgment after mandate is in the lower court. Understand the difference between the decision and mandate to avoid unforced errors.

PRACTICE POINTER

Review with your client the appellate decision after you have a meaningful opportunity to understand the ruling.

C. RESCRIPT

The decision of the appellate court is entitled a "rescript." A rescript is the appellant level equivalent of the trial court's judgment. The rescript provides directions to the lower court for further action consistent with the appellate court's judgment. This can include a remand with instructions to the trial court, a reversal of the trial court, or an affirmance of the trial court's judgment.

In addition, the rescript or the mandate removes the appeals court's jurisdiction over the matter. Similar to how the appellate court took jurisdiction over the matter by the entry of the appeal, it now returns jurisdiction back to the trial court.

Let's examine remaining options after receiving the decisions issued by the appellate court

D. AFFIRMANCE

Let's start with the simplest result issued by the appellate court: affirmance. When you receive an affirmance from the appellate court, the lower court's judgment is confirmed.

If you are the appellee, then you have won the matter.

Your next job is to return the matter back to the trial court for compliance with the trial court's judgment.

Take the example where you represent a wife who receives 100 percent of the proceeds of a sale of the former marital home in the trial court's judgment. The husband appeals the trial court judgment and the order selling the former marital home is stayed pending the appeal.

Once the appellate court affirms the trial court's judgment, the matter needs to be returned by rescript to the trial court and thereafter you can seek compliance of the judgment to sell the former marital home.

But what if you represent the appellant and the matter has been lost in the appellate court?

You have three options to discuss with your now unhappy client: accepting the judgment, petition for rehearing, or appealing to your state's supreme court, if applicable.

Practice Pointer

Explore all remaining options for your client after issuance of the appellate decision.

E. ACCEPTING THE JUDGMENT AND MOVING ON

Discuss with your client the possibility of accepting the appellate court's judgment and ending the matter. This is never an easy conversation. Your client has now lost twice and likely has had enough of you and your legal bills. It is an important option to explore with your client regardless of feelings.

Discuss the high probability against potential future success. This is particularly true when confronted with an "unpublished" decision where it is necessary to seek further review from your state's highest court.

Point out the additional costs to your recalcitrant client who is not accepting the appellate court's judgment.

Discuss with your client that accepting the appellate court's affirmance is a choice.

There is real value psychologically and otherwise in choosing to move on. You have fought the good fight and taken the matter as far as it can go. Closure is an option.

Practice Pointer

If necessary, put in writing your views on accepting the judgment for your client.

But what if the battle should go on?

There are limited circumstances to challenge an appellate court's affirmance of the lower court's judgment in a family matter. For example, a split of authority in state appellate courts on the standard for a removal of a child out of state by one parent.

If your issue is of high legal importance and the appellate court rules against your client, then it may be worthy to seek further appellate review.

There are two afforded options to seek further review. First, you can seek a rehearing in front of the appellate court that issued the decision. Certainly, a long odd against success but depending upon local rule it is an option to be explored with your client.

F. PETITION FOR REHEARING

You need to file a petition for rehearing with the appeals clerk within the required time period. The time afforded is usually ten to twenty days. For example, the Massachusetts rule is fourteen days after the date of the rescript unless the time is shortened or enlarged by order.[134]

The petition must contain points of law or critical fact overlooked or gotten wrong by the appellate court in reaching its decision. It must contain an argument in support of the petition discussing the error of the appellate court. A letter with applicable copies is permitted. But check local rules for required format.

134. Massachusetts Rule Appellate Procedure Rule 27.

Keep in mind action upon a petition for rehearing is afforded great deference and highly unlikely to be granted. Further, if the petition for rehearing is meritless you may end up with an award against your client for reasonable attorney's fees and costs.

Proceed on a petition for rehearing with extreme caution.

PRACTICE POINTER

Only in extreme errors of law or fact should you file a petition for rehearing with the appellate court.

G. PETITION TO SUPREME COURT

The second and more common option is to seek a hearing in your state's highest court. In the event you are seeking review from your state's highest court, your case must have substantial value beyond the immediate interest of your own client. This can include conflicts in state appellate courts, issues of first impression, or novel matters of family law that require a decision by your state's highest court.

The appellate rules afford your client a period of time (twenty days is common) after the date of the rescript to file an application to obtain further appellate review of the case by the state's highest court. Oral argument is afforded only in the rare case where the state supreme court grants the hearing of the petition.[135]

H. CONTENTS

The general required components of a petition for higher appellate review are:

1. A statement requesting leave for further review
2. A statement of case history
3. A concise statement of facts relevant to the appeal
4. A statement of the points that require further appellate review of the decision of the appeals court

135. *Id.*

5. A short argument (no more than ten pages) with supporting appropriate authorities as to why further appellate review is appropriate
6. A copy of the rescript opinion of the appeals court

Follow rules of applicable copies of filing the petition and service of process. For example, the Massachusetts rule requires an original and seventeen copies.[136]

I. OPPOSITION

What if your client is opposing your opponent's further appellate review?

You file an opposition within the allotted time proscribed by the appellate rule for further review. The time frame is generally fairly limited, such as ten days. The opposition *should* contain why the application should be denied. Do not restate your appellate argument.

The decision to file an opposition to a petition for further appellate review is made carefully, as it is not mandatory filing.

Be cognizant of the landscape.

The vast majorities of petitions to your state's highest court are denied.

Further, it is likely if the opposition is strong enough that you will have an opportunity to bring the matter again to your state's high court.

State rules differ as to how many justices are necessary to grant a petition for further review, but if the majority of your state supreme court justices vote in favor, then the petition is granted.

J. ANOTHER BRIEF

Wait, do I have to write another brief?

If you had recognized issues at the beginning of the appellate process as being novel or important, then you followed my advice

136. *Id.*

to write your brief with your state's highest court in mind. Thus you can skip writing a repetitive and new brief.

However, in the event an appellate curveball is in play on an unanticipated legal issue, you can request via motion to your state supreme court permission to rebrief the matter or the supreme court may request further briefing.

Be aware that the state supreme court may impose terms for length of the brief and time for filing, including any response. If a new brief is filed, it is considered in lieu of your original appellate brief.

K. ORAL ARGUMENT

If the petition is granted, then you are back to preparing for another oral argument. An exciting second bite of the apple! Focus particular attention on the issue or issues your state supreme court is raising and conduct your preparation accordingly.

The argument order is the applicant for further appellate review argues first and the respondent to the petition second unless the court orders otherwise.

PRACTICE POINTER

If you are seeking further appellate review, enter into a new fee agreement with your client.

L. REMAND

What if the matter is remanded back to the trial court?

In the event the matter is remanded, then the matter is returned to the jurisdiction of the trial judge to make orders consistent with the appellate court ruling.

Ensure the matter is within the local jurisdiction, after rescript by the appellate court, and then take appropriate action with the court to effectuate the decision.

This may involve scheduling a date for a new trial on the issues flagged or an entire new trial. The lower court is bound to follow the directions and instructions issued by the appellate court. Thus, in a real practical sense, the matter begins again. The complexity depends upon the depth of the orders of the appellate court.

If you are representing the appellant, a remand is generally good news, while if you are the appellee, you are likely dissatisfied with the appellate decision.

PRACTICE POINTER

Obtain a new fee agreement and retainer if the matter is remanded.

M. REVERSAL

A reversal is an equivalent of hitting the family law appellate court jackpot. This is when the appellate court overturns the judgment of the trial judge. This results in a complete "reversal of fortune" and ends the matter with a new prevailing party.

If you are the victorious party, then you return to the trial judge to effectuate the appellate decision, if necessary. For example, if you represent a husband who has been awarded the former marital home, then you now return to the trial court to ensure the appellate order is effectuated.

N. DISMISSAL

The final outcome is an outright dismissal of an appeal.

There are a variety of reasons why an appellate court can dismiss the matter. An appellant fails to prosecute the matter by not filing a brief or by failing to properly comply with local rules of appellate practice.

In the event the appeal is dismissed, ensure the matter is returned to the lower court for jurisdiction. Let's illustrate why it is important that jurisdiction be returned to the lower court for your client.

Take an example of a pro se opponent appealing a monetary judgment for past child support owed to your client. The opposing party obtains a stay of the judgment pending the appeal. Interest adds up on your client's judgment while your opponent remains under the jurisdiction of the appellate court. However, after the required time, he fails to prosecute the appeal and the appellate court issues a dismissal of his appeal.

You need to ensure the matter is out of the appellate court and returned to the trial court to seek compliance of the monetary judgment.

Most states prescribe rules where after a short period of time after dismissal the appellate court relinquishes jurisdiction. You are now free to enforce the judgment in the lower court.

Another example is an award of attorneys' fees. Take the same example from above.

You seek attorneys' fees from the appellate court from your pro se opponent. The appellate court awards your fees and returns the matter to the trial judge. You need to ensure the award of attorneys' fees is enforceable by the trial judge. Ask the appeals court, in your request for attorney fees, to allow the trial judge to enforce any order of attorney fees.

O. CLOSING THE FILE

Once the matter is finally over, it is essential to notify your client and close your file, whatever the outcome of your appeal.

Inform your client, verbally and in writing, that his or her file is now closed in your office. No further work will be commenced, and send a final bill, if applicable.

Make arrangements for storage of files or provide your client with his or her case file at the end of your representation.

Appellate practice is a long, windy road and it is important that clients understand your representation is over.

PRACTICE POINTER

Inform your client in writing your representation is ended win, lose, or draw.

P. A FINAL THOUGHT

An appeal is an attempt at righting a perceived wrong for your client. It is an uphill fight against an imperfect system administered by human beings. Human beings issuing judgments afforded broad discretion by other human beings overlooking those judgments. Judgments made over people's most intimate matters and disputes.

It is complicated in the end.

Justice for one party may not be justice for the other party.

Many times, you are right and *all* the courts just get it wrong. You are likely to lose more of these battles than those you win. A powerful logical argument is not necessarily a winning one.

As human beings are imperfect, so is the law. Families are never easy. And the appellate practice of family law is likewise not easy. Many times results derived from family disputes are wrong despite best efforts.

But results are beside the point.

There is beauty and wisdom in a well-written losing brief.

Your job is to create and find the beauty in the wisdom contained in all of your arguments. For those noble efforts, you are always rewarded win, lose or draw.

Table of Location for Appellate Court Information by State

ALABAMA

Alabama Rules of Appellate Procedure
http://judicial.alabama.gov/Appellate/Index
http://judicial.alabama.gov/library/AppellateProcedure

ALASKA

Alaska Rules of Appellate Procedure
www.appellate.courts.state.ak.us
https://public.courts.alaska.gov/web/rules/docs/app.pdf

ARIZONA

Arizona Rules of Civil Appellate Procedure. Two divisions:
www.azcourts.gov/coa1/
www.appeals2.az.gov/apl2.cfm
https://govt.westlaw.com/azrules/Browse/Home/Arizona/ArizonaCourtRules/ArizonaStatutesCourtRules?guid=N0854C3F0715611DAA16E8D4AC7636430&originationContext=documenttoc&transitionType=Default&contextData=(sc.Default)

ARKANSAS

Rules of Civil Appellate Procedure Civil
https://www.arcourts.gov/courts/court-of-appeals
https://courts.arkansas.gov/rules-and-administrative-orders/rules-of-appellate-procedure—civil

CALIFORNIA

Title Eight Appellate Rules (Rules 8.1–8.1125)
http://appellatecases.courtinfo.ca.gov/
http://www.courts.ca.gov/courtsofappeal.htm

COLORADO

Colorado Appellate Rules
https://www.courts.state.co.us/Courts/Court_Of_Appeals/Index.cfm
https://www.courts.state.co.us/Courts/Court_of_Appeals/Forms_Policies.cfm

CONNECTICUT

Rules of Appellate Procedure
http://jud.ct.gov/appellatecourt/
http://jud.ct.gov/Publications/Handbook_Ap_proc.pdf

DELAWARE

Rules of the Supreme Court of the State of Delaware
https://courts.delaware.gov/superior/
https://courts.delaware.gov/rules/index.aspx#superior

DISTRICT OF COLUMBIA

Rules of Appellate Procedure

https://www.dccourts.gov/court-of-appeals

https://www.dccourts.gov/court-of-appeals/administrative-orders

FLORIDA

Florida Rules of Appellate Procedure
http://www.flcourts.org/florida-courts/district-court-appeal.stml
https://www.floridabar.org/wp-content/uploads/2017/10/Appellate-Court-Rules-10-01-17.pdf

GEORGIA

Court of Appeals Rules
http://www.gaappeals.us/
http://www.gaappeals.us/rules2/index.php

HAWAII

Hawaii Rules of Appellate Procedure
http://www.courts.state.hi.us/opinions_and_orders
http://www.courts.state.hi.us/docs/court_rules/rules/hrap.htm

IDAHO

Idaho Appellate Rules
http://www.isc.idaho.gov:80/mguide/appellate.html
https://isc.idaho.gov/iar

ILLINOIS

Illinois Civil Appellate Procedure
http://www.illinoiscourts.gov/AppellateCourt/default.asp
http://www.illinoiscourts.gov/AppellateCourt/AppGenInfo Default.asp

INDIANA

Indiana Rules of Court—Rules of Appellate Procedure
http://www.in.gov/judiciary/appeals/
http://www.in.gov/judiciary/rules/appellate/index.html

IOWA

Iowa Rules of Appellate Procedure
https://www.iowacourts.gov/iowa-courts/court-of-appeals/

KANSAS

Kansas Appellate Practice (includes general civil actions, divorce, and parentage) K.S.A. § 20-3001 *et seq.*
Kansas Appellate Practice in Child in Need of Care Cases K.S.A. § 38-2273.
Kansas Appellate Practice in Probate (to include adoptions) K.S.A. §58-2401 *et seq.*
http://www.kscourts.org/kansas-courts/court-of-appeals/default.asp

KENTUCKY

Kentucky Supreme Court Rules and Procedure
https://courts.ky.gov/courts/coa/Pages/coa.aspx
https://courts.ky.gov/courts/supreme/Pages/rulesprocedures.aspx

LOUISIANA

Uniform Rules of Louisiana Courts of Appeal
http://www.la-fcca.org/
http://www.la2nd.org/
http://www.la3circuit.org/
http://www.la4th.org/

http://www.fifthcircuit.org/
http://www.la-fcca.org/pdf/20141101UniformRulesCourtsofAppealWeb.pdf

MAINE

Maine Rules of Appellate Procedure
http://www.courts.maine.gov/maine_courts/supreme/appeals.html

MARYLAND

https://www.courts.state.md.us/coappeals

MASSACHUSETTS

Massachusetts Rules of Appellate Procedure
https://www.mass.gov/orgs/appeals-court
https://www.mass.gov/appeals-court-rules-and-standing-orders
https://www.mass.gov/lists/massachusetts-rules-of-appellate-procedure

MICHIGAN

Michigan Court Rules of 1985-Chapter 7 Appellate Rules
http://courts.mi.gov/courts/coa/Pages/default.aspx
http://courts.mi.gov/Courts/MichiganSupremeCourt/rules/Documents/HTML/CRs/Ch%207/Court%20Rules%20Book%20Ch%207-Responsive%20HTML5/index.html#t=Court_Rules_Book_Ch_7%2FCourt_Rules_Chapter_7%2FCourt_Rules_Chapter_7.htm

MINNESOTA

Rules of Civil Appellate Procedure
http://www.mncourts.gov/CourtOfAppeals.aspx

http://www.mncourts.gov/About-The-Courts/SupremeCourt/CourtRules.aspx
http://www.mncourts.gov/CourtOfAppeals/COAHelpTopics.aspx#tab08COAMediation

MISSISSIPPI

Mississippi Rules of Appellate Procedure

https://courts.ms.gov/index.php
https://courts.ms.gov/aboutcourts/aboutthecourts.php

MISSOURI

Rule 84—Procedure in All Appellate Courts
https://www.courts.mo.gov/page.jsp?id=261
https://www.courts.mo.gov/page.jsp?id=993

MONTANA

Appellate Procedure
http://courts.mt.gov/Courts
http://courts.mt.gov/courts/rules/supreme

NEBRASKA

Supreme Court Rules
https://supremecourt.nebraska.gov/courts/court-appeals
https://supremecourt.nebraska.gov/supreme-court-rules

NEVADA

Nevada Rules of Appellate Procedure
https://nvcourts.gov/Supreme/Court_Information/Court_of_Appeals/

https://nvcourts.gov/Supreme/Court_Information/Court_of_Appeals/#

NEW HAMPSHIRE

Rules of the Supreme Court of the State of New Hampshire-Procedural Rules
https://www.courts.state.nh.us/supreme/index.htm
https://www.courts.state.nh.us/rules/scr/index.htm

NEW JERSEY

New Jersey Appellate Court Rules
https://www.njcourts.gov/courts/appellate.html?lang=eng
https://www.njcourts.gov/attorneys/assets/appellate/appellate standards.pdf

NEW MEXICO

New Mexico Rules of Appellate Procedure
https://coa.nmcourts.gov/
https://coa.nmcourts.gov/forms-and-rules.aspx

NEW YORK

Court of Appeals State of New York, Part 500. Rules Of Practice, 22 NYCRR Part 500
http://www.nycourts.gov/ctapps/
http://www.nycourts.gov/ctapps/500rules.htm

NORTH CAROLINA

North Carolina Rules of Appellate Procedure
https://www.nccourts.gov/courts/court-of-appeals
https://www.nccourts.gov/courts/court-of-appeals/about-the-court-of-appeals

NORTH DAKOTA

North Dakota Rules of Appllate Procedure
http://www.ndcourts.gov/
http://www.ndcourts.gov/rules/appellat/frameset.htm

OHIO

Twelve Districts
http://www.sconet.state.oh.us/JudSystem/districtCourts/default.asp
http://www.hamiltoncountyohio.gov/cms/One.aspx?portalId=6254867
http://www.sconet.state.oh.us/JudSystem/districtCourts/district2/default.asp
http://www.sconet.state.oh.us/JudSystem/districtCourts/district3/default.asp
http://www.sconet.state.oh.us/JudSystem/districtCourts/district4/default.asp
http://www.sconet.state.oh.us/JudSystem/districtCourts/district5/default.asp
http://www.sconet.state.oh.us/JudSystem/districtCourts/district6/default.asp
http://www.sconet.state.oh.us/JudSystem/districtCourts/district7/default.asp
http://www.sconet.state.oh.us/JudSystem/districtCourts/district8/default.asp
http://www.sconet.state.oh.us/JudSystem/districtCourts/district9/default.asp
http://www.sconet.state.oh.us/JudSystem/districtCourts/district10/default.asp
http://www.sconet.state.oh.us/JudSystem/districtCourts/district11/default.asp
http://www.sconet.state.oh.us/JudSystem/districtCourts/district12/default.asp
http://www.sconet.state.oh.us/LegalResources/Rules/appellate/AppellateProcedure.pdf
Ohio Rules of Appellate Procedure

OKLAHOMA

Oklahoma Supreme Court Rules
http://www.oscn.net/oscn/schome/civilappeals.htm
http://www.oscn.net/applications/oscn/index.asp?ftdb=STOKRU&level=2

OREGON

The Oregon Rules of Appellate Procedure
http://www.courts.oregon.gov/COA/Pages/index.aspx
http://www.courts.oregon.gov/programs/acrs/resources/Pages/current.aspx

PENNSYLVANIA

Pennsylvania Rules of Appellate Procedure Title 210
http://www.pacourts.us/courts/superior-court/

RHODE ISLAND

Article I. Rhode Island Appellate Procedure
https://www.courts.ri.gov/Courts/SupremeCourt/Pages/default.aspx
https://www.courts.ri.gov/Courts/SupremeCourt/Pages/Supreme%20Court%20Rules.aspx
https://www.courts.ri.gov/Courts/SupremeCourt/Supreme%20Court%20Rules/Supreme-Rules-Article1.pdf
https://www.courts.ri.gov/AppellateMediationProgram/Pages/default.aspx

SOUTH CAROLINA

South Carolina Appellate Court Rules
http://www.sccourts.org/appeals/
http://www.sccourts.org/courtReg/index.cfm

SOUTH DAKOTA

Supreme Court Rules
http://ujs.sd.gov/Supreme_Court/default.aspx

TENNESSEE

Tennessee Rules of Appellate Procedure
http://www.tsc.state.tn.us/courts/court-appeals
http://www.tsc.state.tn.us/courts/court-rules/court-appeals-rules

TEXAS

Fourteen Courts
Texas Rules of Appellate Procedure
http://www.txcourts.gov/about-texas-courts/courts-of-appeals/
http://www.txcourts.gov/media/1436367/1-counties-in-each-district-2005.pdf
http://www.txcourts.gov/supreme/
http://www.txcourts.gov/media/1438277/texas-rules-of-appellate-procedure-updated-with-amendments-effective-7117-with-appendices.pdf

UTAH

Utah Rules of Appellate Procedure
https://www.utcourts.gov/courts/coa/
https://www.utcourts.gov/howto/appeals/
https://www.utcourts.gov/resources/rules/urap/

VERMONT

Vermont Rules of Appellate Procedure
https://www.vermontjudiciary.org/supreme-court

https://www.vermontjudiciary.org/sites/default/files/documents/800-00001%20INSTRUCTIONS%20FOR%20APPEALING%20YOUR%20CASE%20TO%20THE%20SUPREME%20COURT.pdf

VIRGINIA

Part Five. The Supreme Court Appendix of Forms
Part Five A. The Court of Appeals Appendix of Forms Part
http://www.courts.state.va.us/courts/cav/home.html
http://www.courts.state.va.us/courts/scv/rulesofcourt.pdf

WASHINGTON

Rules for Appellate Court Administration
http://www.courts.wa.gov/appellate_trial_courts/
http://www.courts.wa.gov/court_rules/?fa=court_rules.state&group=aca

WEST VIRGINIA

http://www.courtswv.gov/supreme-court/index.html
West Virginia Judiciary, Rules of Appellate Procedure: http://www.courtswv.gov/legal-community/court-rules/appellate-procedure/Part-III.html#rule10

WISCONSIN

Wisconsin Court of Appeals—Internal Operating Procedures
https://www.wicourts.gov/courts/appeals/index.htm
https://www.wicourts.gov/ca/IOPCA.pdf
Clerk of the Wisconsin Supreme Court and Court of Appeals, *Guide to Appellate Procedure for the Self-Represented* (2015): https://www.wicourts.gov/publications/guides/docs/proseappealsguide.pdf

WYOMING

Court Rule—Rules of the Supreme Court of Wyoming
https://www.courts.state.wy.us/supreme-court/
https://www.courts.state.wy.us/court_rule/rules-of-the-supreme-court-of-wyoming/

FEDERAL RULES

Federal Rules of Appellate Procedure
http://www.uscourts.gov/rules-policies/current-rules-practice-procedure
http://www.uscourts.gov/sites/default/files/appellate-rules-procedure-dec2017_0.pdf

Practice Pointers

From the Introduction

1. You must know your local rules of appellate practice in your jurisdiction.

From Chapter 1

2. Understand the effect of a post-trial motion on the notice of appeal to preserve your client's appellate rights.
3. If a future modification solves the post-trial problem, it is likely a better avenue than an appeal due to the long odds against a successful appeal.
4. Appeals are more successful when the goals of the client and attorney align.
5. Always inform your client an appeal does not always end with a simple win or a lose.

From Chapter 2

6. Never take an appeal when a client does not have a clear goal to achieve from the appeals court.
7. Always trust but verify what your client and/or trial counsel state what appears in the record.
8. Do not forget the essential goal of any brief is to persuade the appellate court of your theory as to how the lower court made an error and by doing that, and only that, will it ultimately please your client.
9. All fee agreements must be in writing even if it is not required by your local rules.

From Chapter 3

10. Apply the same procedure for considering an appeal of a final judgment to take an interlocutory appeal.
11. Always proceed with extreme caution in determining whether to challenge an order by interlocutory relief, as the relief you seek is extraordinary.
12. An interlocutory appeal is not a substitute for an appeal after final judgment.

From Chapter 4

13. When in doubt, always object to preserve the record.
14. A written argument is better than an oral argument to protect the record.
15. If you make an oral argument, and if time allows it, write it down to ensure all your points make it into the record.
16. Add a footnote on all financial statements stating the financial statement is subject to an update for any unintended errors or omissions.
17. Maintain in your trial binder a list of evidentiary objections to cite a specific rule quickly during trial.
18. Create your findings of fact prior to trial. During trial, check them off as you establish each fact.
19. Use "chalks" to summarize evidence for the trial. But the "chalk" is not evidence per se and the underlying documents and/or exhibits must be submitted into evidence to preserve the record.
20. Have a court stenographer present during a trial if there is a possibility of an appeal.
21. Limit your representation initially to a record review in order to determine the validity of an appeal.

From Chapter 5

22. Identify the standard of review early in your review of the matter.
23. Follow your gut when you consider taking on an appeal for a potential client.

From Chapter 6

24. After receipt of the lower court's judgment, meet with your client to discuss postjudgment motions prior to filing a notice of appeal.
25. If there has been fraudulent conduct by an adverse party, an alternative remedy to a rule 60 motion might be an equity action to divide an undisclosed asset.
26. If you have any doubt as to whether the appeal period has been properly extended as a result of the filing of a motion under rule 52(b) or 59, file a notice of appeal within the required time period regardless. If it is premature, it is void and no harm is done. If the motions did not for some reason stay the appeals period, then you timely filed your notice.
27. If you are likely to appeal an issue and your judge is likely to deny any post-trial relief, an appeal may be the only option.
28. If you are seeking a stay of a judgment and it involves property division, request relief by proposing a sufficient bond pending the appeal.
29. Always file a motion to stay concurrently with all other post-trial motions. Perhaps the judge denies your motions but grant, in whole or in part, the request for a stay.
30. Even when there is no appeal of a judgment, ensure all required findings are entered to preserve a future modification action.

From Chapter 7

31. If there is any confusion as to where to file the notice of appeal, confirm with a clerk of the court.
32. To be safe—file a motion to be permitted to file the appeal even if the motion is untimely under your local rules.
33. A family law notice of appeal should be limited to only the matter you are seeking an appeal of and no ancillary matters.
34. When you first receive a judgment from the lower court, immediately contact the lower court to find out if the judgment has been docketed so you can determine in your initial

conversations with your client how many days you have to file a notice of appeal.

35. When a judgment has not been entered into the docket, consult the clerk to determine when the judgment may enter but also request the judgment is entered on the docket so you can file your notice of appeal.
36. Serve the notice of appeal and file a proof of service even if no rule requires it.
37. File multiple notice of appeals if and when there is uncertainty as to the effective date judgment and/or docket entry.

From Chapter 8

38. Understand the difference between the record of the court and record appendix, which you create to support your brief and submit to the court along with your brief.
39. A stenographer hired for trial can ensure a complete and thorough record.
40. Always read each and every word of the trial transcript even if you were trial counsel.
41. Understand and acknowledge the difference between challenging a judgment and changing a judgment.
42. It is very likely your appeal contains confidential information requiring segregation from other information contained in your brief.

From Chapter 9

43. Think of the record appendix as your offer of proof to the appeals court and is comprised of materials necessary to correct the wrong of the lower court.
44. Create your own appendix of documents, testimony, or evidence you want the appellate court to review and then ensure it is within the record the appeals court is actually reviewing.

From Chapter 10

45. Always start with an outline of the major issues to be challenged, but be flexible to add or alter your outline as you draft.

46. Always develop your theme early and add it to the outline of your brief.
47. The weight of authority is determined by its reasoning in its ruling.
48. Be aware of emerging trends in the law when they are relevant to your case and use them to support your argument.
49. Read books on the art of writing, and if you find one difficult to read, discard it immediately.
50. Write your brief in a clear, direct, and consistent manner.
51. Use the facts without emotion and in a direct, matter-of-fact manner to tell your client's story.
52. Avoid being overly academic in your brief. Instead focus on the facts and your legal reasoning to make your argument.
53. If your case is of first impression or even novel, then write your brief assuming it makes it to your state's supreme court.
54. After you draft the outline and before you begin drafting your brief, take time to read a well-written brief in the same topic area.

From Chapter 11

55. Check your state's appellate website for format requirements.
56. Maintain your own checklist to prepare and draft your brief to ensure compliance with local rules.
57. Always file your brief twenty-four hours in advance of any deadline to confirm your brief was properly submitted and to allow time to correct any deficiencies.
58. Always register with your appeals court if electronic filings are permitted to save time and money for the production of briefs. It is also the trend across the country in appellate practice. Do not get left behind.
59. In matters of interstate custody, an expedited appeal must always be seriously considered.
60. Do not wait until the last minute to file a motion for enlargement of time. It saves time to plan ahead and determine when you can realistically submit your brief.
61. You are likely to be granted an extension of time to file your brief, but take the motion seriously and provide sufficient detail to ensure the court grants your motion to extend time for filing of your brief.

From Chapter 12

62. Have a good proofreader for every brief you write to check not only format but also your citations.
63. Less is more in determining the statement of your issues on appeal.
64. You should be a great storyteller, and arranging how you tell the tale is a critical component to writing an excellent brief.
65. Be prepared to confront negative facts at all stages of the appellate process.
66. When writing the statement of facts, ensure that by the time your reader finishes, they want to know what happens next when you apply the law to your argument.
67. Write the summary of your argument only after you have written your argument.
68. Always be eloquently brief in your argument.
69. Leave no doubt as to what you are seeking from the appellate court.
70. Ask for attorney fees and costs any time you are responding to a less-than-meritorious brief.
71. Always present any document to the appeals court in the most reader-friendly manner in compliance with your local rules.

From Chapter 13

72. When you represent the appellee, take every opportunity to support the trial court's judgment.
73. Make a checklist to ensure compliance with all requirements of your jurisdiction for an appellee brief.
74. Always directly confront your opponent's strongest arguments.
75. Never make it personal in any brief.
76. Treat a pro se writer of an appellant brief the same as you would treat a brief written by experienced counsel.

From Chapter 14

77. Do not use the reply brief to repeat your arguments when your opponent failed to respond to them in the responsive brief.

From Chapter 15

78. Know the rules of oral argument at the beginning of your written brief preparation.
79. Your time allowed for oral argument will go fast.
80. Pay attention to time but pay more attention to the chief justice to dictate when you are out of time.
81. Always avoid inserting yourself in a family law dispute where you could be considered a witness at every stage of the litigation.

From Chapter 16

82. Never underestimate the importance of oral argument.
83. View oral argument as your opportunity to provide a humanistic perspective to your legal argument.

From Chapter 17

84. Your preparation instills the confidence necessary for an effective oral argument.
85. Do not rely on a junior associate for your understanding of the facts. Be personally familiar with all factors of your case.
86. Use your brief outline to help formulate your outline for oral argument.
87. Outstanding preparation for oral argument makes the difference between an average presentation and a presentation your client deserves.
88. As part of your preparation, focus on developing a single sentence defining your argument.
89. Be familiar with the room where you are arguing.
90. Register with the appeals court of your jurisdiction to receive all decisions issued or have a system in place to receive all opinions as adjudicated.

From Chapter 18

91. Always arrive early for oral argument—at least ninety minutes before is a good rule of thumb.
92. Be minimalistic in what you bring to the podium.

From Chapter 19

93. Never respond to a question from the appellate court with a guess.
94. Always listen very carefully to the court's questions and respond directly.
95. No matter what, do not let the panelists see you sweat.
96. Sometimes, one major point is enough to win your argument.
97. Adhere to your theory of the case and do not concede it under any circumstances.

From Chapter 20

98. Review with your client the appellate decision after you have a meaningful opportunity to understand the ruling.
99. Explore all remaining options for your client after issuance of the appellate decision.
100. If necessary, put in writing your views on accepting the judgment for your client.
101. Only when there are extreme errors of law or fact should you file a petition for rehearing with the appellate court.
102. If you are seeking further appellate review, enter into a new fee agreement with your client.
103. Obtain a new fee agreement and retainer if the matter is remanded.
104. Inform your client in writing your representation is ended win, lose, or draw.

Fundamental Rules for Confidential Information

1. Rule 1: Use extreme caution in protecting confidential information in the record, the brief, and your record appendix.
2. Rule 2: Avoid the name of children or party names in your brief.
3. Rule 3: Always protect personal identifying information (PII).
4. Redact when you have any concern with the use of confidential information.

Commandments for Reply Briefs

1. **When you are the appellant you almost always file a reply brief**
2. **Your reply brief is a direct answer to your opponent's brief**
3. **Leave out your weak arguments in your reply brief**
4. Your reply brief focuses on what is critical in the appellee's brief
5. Maintain credibility in your reply to the court
6. **Provide your theory of the case again**
7. **Do not be boring in your reply brief**
8. Make your reply brief "brief"
9. **Pay attention to the details in your reply brief**
10. **Inform the court of exactly what you want,** again

Objectives of Oral Argument

1. To answer all questions and remove all doubt
2. To reinforce the argument and logic of your brief
3. Address your theme
4. To demonstrate you are thoughtful and correctly applied the facts to the law
5. Show your likeability and fairness
6. Never miss a thing

The Appellate Checklist for Your Family Law Appeal

INITIAL

- ☐ All other possibilities have been explored prior to proceeding.
- ☐ The appeal has both a clear and realistic goal.
- ☐ Client is fully informed of the appellate process.
- ☐ Client is aware of the odds against the success of an appeal (if the client is the appellant).
- ☐ A written fee agreement has been executed.

THE RECORD

- ☐ Review the trial court's judgment.
- ☐ Review findings to support the trial court's judgment.
- ☐ Collect the record to review.
- ☐ Order transcripts, if applicable.
- ☐ Review the record.
- ☐ Make sure assembly of the record is complete.

NOTICE OF APPEAL

- ☐ Review any appellate time deadlines.
- ☐ Review any effect on the timing of the notice of appeal of any filed post-trial motions.

- ☐ Notice of appeal has been filed.
- ☐ File new notice of appeal, if applicable due to post-trial motions.
- ☐ Ensure appeal is entered on the appellate court docket.

DETERMINE THE ERROR

- ☐ Set out the legal error.
- ☐ Set out relief the client is asking.
- ☐ Standard of review has been examined.
- ☐ An error or law?
- ☐ An abuse of discretion?

THE RECORD APPENDIX

- ☐ Prepare the Record Appendix.
- ☐ Protect confidential information into a separate Record Appendix.

BRIEF WRITING

- ☐ Review local jurisdiction requirements.
- ☐ Outline your brief.
- ☐ Identify key facts.
- ☐ Identify key case law and pertinent statutes.
- ☐ Find general proposition support from other sources, if necessary.
- ☐ Draft initial brief.

FORMAT BRIEF

- ☐ Check for proper format as citations.
- ☐ Edit brief.
- ☐ Client discussion.

- ☐ Trial counsel discussion, if applicable.
- ☐ Final brief.

FILING SUBMISSIONS

- ☐ Recheck submission requirements.
- ☐ Final original documents to be filed.
- ☐ Determine type of filing: hand-deliver or e-filing.
- ☐ Prepare required copies of filings.
- ☐ Create Certificate of Service.
- ☐ File.

THE REPLY BRIEF

- ☐ Determine, if necessary to file
- ☐ Select key areas to attack.
- ☐ Outline.
- ☐ Initial draft.
- ☐ Final draft.
- ☐ Check filing requirements.
- ☐ File.

ORAL ARGUMENT

- ☐ Review Record Appendix.
- ☐ Review all briefs.
- ☐ Review key case law.
- ☐ Review key statutes.
- ☐ Determine opening.
- ☐ Determine theme.
- ☐ Outline.
- ☐ Conduct mock court.

CLIENT REVIEW

- ☐ Provide thoughts to client.

AFTER DECISION

- ☐ Determine next steps, if any.
- ☐ Remand.
- ☐ Higher court review.
- ☐ Inform the client.
- ☐ Close file.

Acknowledgments

There are a number of people who I must recognize for making the writing of this book possible. A huge thank you to my wonderful children, Jacob and Jenna. They both inspire me daily. They also pushed me to shave my "unruly beard" that compelled me to finally complete the very first draft.

I am fortunate to work with talented lawyers who provided me with valuable assistance and who gave their own time and energy to help me clean up my many early drafts. I am grateful for the contributions of Attorney Jennifer "Top Dog" Salerno and Attorney Claire Frantz for the creation of this work.

A big thank you for support goes to the "Princess of the Probate Court" Attorney Kirsten Demoga. Thank you for choosing to practice with me.

A long overdue thank you to my law school roommate, Attorney Joseph Levin, for his encouragement "many moons ago" that I could, in fact, write a book. Better late than never.

A huge thank you to the editorial assistance and extreme patience for the production of this book goes to Sarah Busche and Joseph Booth of the American Bar Association and the Family Law Section. They both made immeasurable contributions to this book and made me a better writer.

A thank you to my mother and my father for being wonderful people and parents and for the full encouragement and support along the way.

Finally, the biggest thank you of all to my wife, Beth, my true partner and love of my life. I could not have gotten this done without her. As any divorce lawyer knows well, "the happy wife equals the happy life."

Acknowledgments

About the Author

Matthew P. Barach is a family law trial attorney and appellate family law specialist in Massachusetts. He is the founder and principal of Barach Family Law Group, LLC, a law firm devoted to excellence in family law.

He is a Phi Beta Kappa graduate of Clark University and the recipient of the H. Donaldson Jordan Prize (1992) for excellence in writing. He is a graduate of the University of California, Hastings College of the Law.

He appears regularly before the Massachusetts Appeals Court, the Massachusetts Supreme Judicial Court, and the First Circuit of Appeals. He was on the winning side and responsible for two of the most important landmark family law cases case in the Commonwealth pertaining to alimony and child custody.

He is responsible for a number of articles in family law. Among them are "A Mistrial in the Probate Court" in *Massachusetts Family Law Journal* (2016) and "The Importance of Exigent Circumstances Supporting Temporary Orders in Modification Actions in the Probate Court," in *Massachusetts Family Law Journal* (2016).

He regularly is granted the highest Avvo.com distinction and has been rated as a top 10 family law attorney in Massachusetts and a top 100 Lawyer in America by various rating organizations. He is considered by many attorneys "the fixer" in family law in the Commonwealth.

He is an avid golfer who lives with his children and wife in the suburbs of Boston. He hopes to someday appear before the U.S. Supreme Court in a family law appeal.

Index

S